1-38

ABSTRACTS AND ABSTRACTING SERVICES

By the Same Author

DICTIONARIES OF ENGLISH AND FOREIGN LANGUAGES

INDEXES AND INDEXING

BIBLIOGRAPHIES, SUBJECT AND NATIONAL

ENCYCLOPAEDIAS, THEIR HISTORY THROUGHOUT THE AGES

BOOK COLLECTING

INFORMATION SERVICES

LIBRARY ASSISTANCE TO READERS

COMMERCIAL AND INDUSTRIAL RECORDS STORAGE

BIBLIOGRAPHICAL SERVICES THROUGHOUT THE WORLD (UNESCO)

INDEXING BOOKS

NEWNES DICTIONARY OF DATES

BRITISH BROADCASTING: A READER'S GUIDE

MODERN BUSINESS FILING AND ARCHIVES

A JORROCKS HANDBOOK

THE SCOLMA DIRECTORY OF LIBRARIES AND COLLECTIONS ON AFRICA

DIRECTORY OF LIBRARIES AND SPECIAL COLLECTIONS ON ASIA AND NORTH AFRICA

(Editor) THE ANNALS OF ABSTRACTING, 1665–1970

PROGRESS IN LIBRARY SCIENCE

ABSTRACTS AND ABSTRACTING SERVICES

By

ROBERT COLLISON

Fellow of the Library Association

Santa Barbara, California   Oxford, England

1971

© 1971
by
Robert Collison

Library of Congress Catalog Card No. 78-149635
SBN Paperbound Edition 0-87436-079-X
Clothbound Edition 0-87436-078-1

Printed and bound in the United States of America

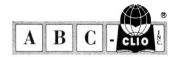

American Bibliographical Center—Clio Press

Riviera Campus, 2040 Alameda Padre Serra
Santa Barbara, California
Oxford, England

To the Members of the First Seminar on
Abstracts and Abstracting Services, 1969,
Graduate School of Library Service,
University of California, Los Angeles:

Carol Bedoian
Julia J. Gotthold
Willem J. Hamer
Terry E. Hubbard
Hilja Kukk
Cheryl Sanford
Mary Lynn Vickers
Judy Waldron

Le dessein de ce Journal estant de faire sçavoir ce qui se passe de nouveau dans la Republique des lettres . . .

Je crois qu'il y a peu de personnes qui ne voient que ce Journal sera utile à ceux qui acheptent des Livres; puis qu'ils ne le feront point sans les connoistre auparavant: & qu'il ne sera pas inutile à ceux mesme qui ne peuvent faire beaucoup de despense en Livres, puis que sans les achepter, ils ne laisseront pas d'en avoir une connoissance generale. Ceux qui ent entrepris ce Journal ont long-temps douté s'ils devoient le donner tous les ans, tous les mois, ou toutes les semaines. Mais enfin ils ont crû qu'il devoit paroistre chaque semaine: parce que les choses vieilliroient trop, si on differoit d'en parlor pendant l'espace d'un an ou d'un mois . . .

Ainsi sans rien changer au jugement d'un chacun, il se donnera seulement la liberté de changer quelquefois l'expression: & il n'espousera aucun party. Cette indifference sans doute sera jugée necessaire, dans un Ouvrage qui ne doit pas estre moins libre de toute sorte de prejugez, qu'exempt de passion & de partialité.

"L'Imprimeur au lecteur," *Le Journal des sçavans,* Monday, 5th January, 1665

CONTENTS

INTRODUCTION

Most abstracting services have started without any statement of the motives that underlay their inception, and without any outline of the policies ruling their approach and coverage. At least, these do not appear in their original issues, though it is probable that they may have been sketched in the promotional material that heralded their publication. Occasionally, one is fortunate as in the case of the first issue of *Abstracts for Social Workers,* issued in Spring 1965 by the National Association of Social Workers. On the verso of the title page of Volume 1, number 1, of this abstracting service we find a statement that is worth reprinting in full:

> The inauguration of *Social Work Abstracts* is a happy and auspicious event. The journal represents a milestone in the development of a knowledge base for the social work profession. The abstracts will not in themselves produce knowledge, but they should help overcome certain obstacles which have limited the development of knowledge in the past.
>
> Prior to 1955, social work practice was developed in separate fields and fragmented among seven separate organizations. It lacked the frames of reference and systematically organized theoretical propositions necessary for structured thought, as well as proper channels for continuous intellectual effort and theory building. In spite of creative contributions from many individuals, the thinking and writing about practice reflected in social work literature were not cumulative because most of the writers tended to start fresh from their own experience and to limit their analysis to single instances.
>
> In the early fifties an important change took place. The growing conviction that a common base existed for all social work practice led to the formation of a single professional association. The much-needed channel for comprehensive examination of practice was at last provided. It finally became possible to undertake consistent analysis and study on a cumulative basis.
>
> The role of *Social Work Abstracts* in such a continuing effort is apparent. The abstracts should not only be of substantial aid in synthesizing existing social work knowledge, but should also stimulate research in practice necessary to develop the knowledge dimension. The abstracts service makes possible two new developments in the field. First social work practitioners and teachers will be able to follow quickly innovations in the diagnosis and treatment of social problems. Second, the formulation of a classification scheme should help break the barrier, hitherto insurmountable of codifying social work literature.
>
> The basic objective of the abstracts service is to improve the quality of social work practice. The rapid and accurate communication of professional knowledge made possible by the abstracts supplies an important ingredient for the accomplishment of this objective. Its ultimate achievement may in great measure be related to the stimulus to practice this journal provides.

This straightforward and moving statement, made by Dr. David Fanshel, Chairman of the Editorial Advisory Board, typifies—I believe—the motivation behind the foundation of a great many abstracting services. The advantages of such aids to rapid and accurate information are clear and it seems probable that the delay in the inception of a large number of abstracting services was more likely to be due to lack of finances than to lack of interest. With a history of formal publication of at least three centuries, and a pre-history of at least a thousand years, abstracts have a fascination that grows as one pursues the numerous side paths to which even the slightest study of the subject inevitably leads.

The present volume is a pioneer effort, with all the faults and omissions that that implies. But it is hoped that one of the outcomes will be the contribution of much more knowledge concerning the background of abstracts and abstracting services. Certainly, many people have provided items and ideas from their own knowledge and experience that have been incorporated in this book. I am especially grateful for the help and encouragement I have received from Mrs. Johanna E. Tallman, Librarian, Engineering and Mathematical Sciences Library; Dr. Harold Borko, Professor of Library Service; and Miss Louise Darling, Assistant University Librarian, Biomedical Library, at UCLA; Mrs. H. W. Horn, of the ERIC Clearinghouse for Junior College Information; and to Dr. Eric Boehm and Mr. Lloyd Garrison at ABC-Clio Press; in addition to many other colleagues who have been kind enough to discuss at length points of detail concerning abstracts and their uses. I must, however, emphasize that any errors are of my own making, and that I shall welcome comments, criticisms, and—especially—additional information that can help to improve future editions.

R.C.

UCLA
15 May, 1971

DEFINITIONS, PURPOSE AND COSTS

Since no one has ever defined a good abstract, the future of abstracting, professional or amateur, seems assured.

L. VANBY

No current dictionary appears to be able to define modern abstracts in terms that would be acceptable to their users. Various sources equate an abstract with an epitome, a synopsis, or a summary—and, added to these, other near-related words might also be considered synonyms, such as abridgment, précis, paraphrase, digest, or even "the gist of an argument." But an abstract in its modern sense is none of these. An epitome is a brief statement of the chief points of significance; a synopsis is a general view or statement, and it can comprise a series of headings or an outline; a summary is similar to an epitome, but often occupies a place at the end of a statement or report; an abridgment is a reduction of the original document that may omit a number of secondary points; a précis gives only the essential points; a paraphrase is a kind of interpretation in one's own language; a digest is usually a methodically arranged presentation of the arguments; and, such as an author might submit of his new novel or for a film; the gist is the hub or pith of the matter usually demanded by the impatient urging: "Get to the point, man!"

But an abstract does not fall into any of these categories. It is the terse presentation in (as far as possible) the author's own language, of all the points made, in the same order as in the original piece of primary documentary information—and that can be a book, a research report, a periodical article, a speech, the proceedings of a conference, an interview, etc. It is much more than this, too, for it is intended to stand as a readable and complete item in its own right, and is therefore a separate work of scholarship that can be fully indexed and exploited for the benefit of scholars and research workers.

It is tempting to say that the vast majority of the world's population is

3

unaware of the existence of abstracts (or at least unable to recognize them at sight) and seems to be managing without their help without apparent difficulty. This would be misleading, for the world at large is affected by abstracts in many features of everyday life, even though their benefits are obvious only to the specialist. Abstracts are a documentary tool that need to be used if work is not to be duplicated or misdirected or delayed. Abstracts are in fact part of the day-to-day life of modern scholarship and research, and they are growing rapidly in volume, in coverage, and in effectiveness.

What is the purpose of making an abstract of something that already exists? To a certain extent there are parallels in the world of ordinary life. At a shop specializing in selling wall-paper, there will be pattern books that show in a comparatively small area *every* detail of each pattern that appears on the complete sheet. Those who look through these patterns know that when they receive the rolls of wall-paper there will be no surprises in this respect, for the pattern has shown the complete range of variation in detail. Similarly, in many other spheres, the support for a bed, the angle-support for book-shelves, etc., can be inspected in model compact form, so that a clear idea can be gained of their suitability for a particular task. In the same way, the abstract of a piece of documentary material will—if it has been thoroughly done—give the reader exact and concise knowledge of the total content of the very much more lengthy original, so that he can judge whether he needs to consult the full text. It has been known to draw to the reader's attention points that had escaped him when he first read the complete item. It should be added however that some items do not lend themselves to treatment of this kind, and for such works a descriptive form of abstract is substituted that merely indicates what the item is about. This form will be defined and discussed in detail later.

In these days of various systems of quicker reading, in which users of documentary material are becoming experts in the art of glancing rapidly through large quantities of print, are such things as abstracts really necessary? After all, one does not have to eat the whole of a cake to find out whether one likes it. But the truth is that what is somewhat sensationally called the "information explosion" has been taking place for several centuries and that advanced forms of exploitation of knowledge such as abstracts and computerized indexing are needed if the world is to benefit at the earliest time possible from what *has* been discovered, what *is* being discovered, and what is on the brink of discovery or at least under intensive research. In the English language alone some fifty thousand books are published each year, and over fifty thousand periodicals are also being issued. Add to these figures the far higher estimates for the other languages of the world—publications in both the Russian and the Chinese languages individually exceed these figures—and it will be seen that if a man sat down all day long and merely turned the pages of contemporary publications at speed without glancing at their contents, he could only account for a small fraction of this output.

Similarly, within a given subject-field, the most zealous pursuer of his craft could not possibly read everything that has been written on his subject, even if he devoted his entire waking life to this and to nothing else. It is well known, for example, that doctors find difficulty in keeping up with developments in the field of medicine, but far greater difficulties are experienced by chemists, physicists, biologists, and most scientists and technologists. It might of course be argued that the advance of knowledge in any sector is painfully slow and that most of the material published is largely a rehash or a reworking of what is already known, but a glance at the International Federation for Documentation's *Abstracting Services in Science, Technology, Medicine, Agriculture, Social Sciences, Humanities* (The Hague, 1969) will show that this is not really so, and when it is considered that a new edition of that list would probably need to be one-and-a-half times its present size, it is clear that however repugnant it may be to the research worker to know that the very act of reading abstracts further reduces the already limited time he had for reading original material in his field, no satisfactory alternative exists if his work is to progress. In any case, the reader's real aim is to keep up with his subject rather than master the contents of so many periodicals, and the abstract journal is logically his best means of doing this.

This problem, though it has come much to the fore in the past twenty years, is no new one. Abstracts, as will be seen from the outline of their history (pp. 59-64), have a long ancestry, and—at least from the very beginning of printing, if not long before—mankind knew that something of the sort would be necessary. The present insistence on the importance of abstracts and abstracting is however largely due to the rapid increase in scientific and technological advance in this and the last centuries. Thus, although abstracts are needed in all branches of knowledge, they have come in public estimation to be particularly identified with science and technology. The current growth in the manufacture of abstracts is due also to the expanding capacities of the mechanized information retrieval systems which are now beginning to offer services that would have been almost inconceivable only a few years ago. The two are interactive: for the computer and the magnetic tape or disc to be able to offer these services, they must have the material on which their operations are based presented in such a form that they can handle it mechanically. And writers are being increasingly encouraged to provide abstracts of their work at the time when the latter is submitted, so that its results will be available in mechanized form at least as soon as the full text is published (abstracts are now often issued in advance of the delivery of conference papers). That this is wise will at once be recognized when it is realized that even in these days of the filmsetting of type, etc., there is still great delay in the publication of most work of scholarship or research. Thus abstracts summarize current research for busy people and also give them initial access to the information contained in scarce materials, of which foreign-language items constitute a large share. As Eric Boehm has said: "Languages are a much more serious barrier to research than is commonly assumed, and parochialism in research is much more pronounced than we permit ourselves to believe."*

At the moment some one thousand abstract journals are coping with the contents of some fifty thousand English and foreign-language periodicals. Thus, the great bulk of material still remains to be dealt with. The intellectual proportions, too, are unsatisfactory; most of these abstract journals deal with the scientific and technological fields, though an increasing number are beginning to deal with the various aspects of the enormous area of the social sciences. On the humanities side, the picture is however far less comforting, and it is only recently that any considerable advance has been achieved. Costs are of course largely responsible for this state of affairs: the wide range of scientific and technological abstract journals is supported by industry and commerce and by individual governments because these periodicals are an essential part of the effort to advance business and manufacturing. Since the humanities cannot show such visible returns, financial support for abstracts in this field is rarely forthcoming, and efforts so far are largely due to voluntary public-spirited and practical aid deriving from within the circle of scholars and research workers dealing with these subjects.

The purposes for which abstracts are made have been discussed; the users' purposes in reading them are equally worthy of consideration. It has been found that almost three-fifths of the users are looking for specific information which is directly pertinent to their work in hand, and that over two-fifths use abstracts for keeping abreast of current literature in their primary field of interest, while another but overlapping two-fifths use them for keeping abreast of current literature in fringe subjects of interest. Among rather less than one-fifth of the users, the abstracts are utilized for retrospective reference or information retrieval. When it is remembered that it is the exceptional periodical article that is cited in scientific or technological papers once it is more than five years old, it will be seen that the overwhelming user-interest is in current material, particularly foreign-language material. Thus, the importance of abstracts of English language material in those countries where English is *not* spoken will be fully appreciated.

This being so, it is well to ask the cost of abstracting, for it is certain that this is a figure that increases constantly. It has been estimated that in the United States alone well over two-and-a-half million items are abstracted and indexed annually and while the total cost is not precisely known it is estimated that the cost of indexing an individual item is approximately $7.50, and the cost of abstracting is about $30 per article including, of course, its bibliographical citation. The publishers of *Chemical Abstracts* have estimated the unit cost per abstract at $23-25, including research budgets. Nevertheless, *Biological Abstracts* pointed out in 1968 that the

---

*Quoted (without reference) by Barry S. Brook in "Some new paths for music bibliography" in *Computers in Humanistic Research,* edited by Edmund A. Bowles (New York, Prentice-Hall, 1967, p. 206).

unit cost to the consumer is only 0.0037 cents! The average abstract journal must allocate about half its total budget to the cost of preparing and editing abstracts.

Is it all worth it? The answer is undoubtedly "yes," for the circulation figures for abstract journals steadily increase, though not at such a rate as to help reduce costs to the individual subscribers. The fact is that those libraries which could benefit most from the contents of abstract journals —that is, the smallest libraries which naturally lack files of most of the periodicals abstracted—are the least likely to subscribe. They could of course gain a great deal from abstract journals which provide in a nutshell what the smaller libraries cannot provide in full, and their subscriptions would help reduce the prices of these journals. Gradually the position will right itself; in the meantime, the best libraries will continue to support abstract journals, since they are an essential tool of scholarship and research.

THE WRITERS OF ABSTRACTS

> *The quality of abstracts depends largely on the ability of the abstractor to understand the significance of the paper being covered.*
>
> E.J. CRANE

A question that has never been resolved satisfactorily—and one that will probably remain unanswered—is, who is the right person to write an abstract? Clearly it must be someone who is familiar with the subject of the item to be abstracted and is therefore in a position to understand what needs to be conveyed. This seems to imply that the abstractor should either be the author of the original item or a specialist in the relevant subject field. Of these two, it would appear that the author is preferable since he is probably the only person who fully appreciates the import of what he has written, particularly if his work is a new and original contribution to the subject.

Unfortunately the problem is not as simple as this. It is certain that a number of authors are incapable of writing adequate abstracts of their own work. Just as a composer may not be the best executant of his own compositions, so an author may not be able to do justice to his own writings. An abstract needs to be free of argument and to convey simply—and without bias or embellishment—what has been published. The author, having been intimately involved in the research he describes, may find it difficult to achieve the impersonal and comprehensive lines of an abstract and, his own expert brain, leaping ahead from the first tentative experiments to the final conclusion, may fail to take sufficient care to include *all* the intermediate steps between a theorem and its solution.

Though authors make use of abstracts, it is not always certain that they fully appreciate their value or their specific place in the documentation of knowledge. Thus an author may assume that the provision of an abstract will perhaps prevent some people from reading his original contribution. He may therefore think in terms of writing his abstract as a kind of *bonne* *bouche* that will tempt readers to embark on the full text. While this kind of attitude may appear unreasonable to the observer, it is an important point to keep in mind, for it is unwise to assume that any kind of creator can remain completely objective or unbiased where his own work is concerned. Thus, while Charles L. Bernier says "Abstracting is an art. It can be learned," he also points out that "It is difficult, if not impossible to have all authors become experienced abstractors."*

Turning to the specialist as an abstractor, certain objections immediately become apparent. If the author is making an original contribution to his subject, then his work is in advance of any knowledge hitherto possessed even by specialists. Will the specialist therefore fully appreciate the ideas the author is attempting to convey and himself be able to incorporate them in his abstract? The answer must be that everything depends on the skill of the author, starting from known concepts, in being able to develop by trial and proof new concepts stemming logically from those previously accepted. Here lie both the weakness and the strength of the professional abstractor—he represents the readers as a whole and he must therefore convey the complete range of processes by which the author has arrived at his conclusions if the reader (who has not seen the original contribution) is to understand and appreciate the author's intention. Any omission of a step in the author's working will leave the reader in doubt; any generalization by the abstractor of specific points made by the author will similarly make difficulties for the reader. The degree of seriousness in such omissions can be measured by the possibility of a reader's overlooking something important that has been achieved and recorded in document form.

But if the proposed abstractor is to convey successfully the author's whole intention, it would seem necessary for him to have access to the author and to be able to consult him on any difficult points. This is possible only in a very small number of cases. The likelihood is that the author and the abstractor may be physically separated by hundreds if not thousands of miles. The alternative—the submission of a draft of the abstract to the author—may not be a very useful solution either, since it can delay publication of the abstract, and since it implies that the author's approval is necessary before publication. Moreover, the abstract may be written in a different language from that which the author normally uses. And, if the author is truly creative, by the time he receives the draft of the abstract he will already be busy working on further contributions to knowledge that may prevent his giving more than cursory attention to what the abstractor has written—particularly if he is unconvinced of the value of abstracts as a means of conveying knowledge.

Nevertheless, these are not sufficient arguments to rule out the desirability of authors and abstractors collaborating wherever possible in the

---

Encyclopedia of Library and Information Science, edited by Allen Kent and Harold Lancour (New York, Marcel Dekker, 1968. Volume 1, pp. 16-38: "Abstracts and abstracting").

drafting of adequate abstracts. It is simply that it is important to keep these considerations in mind and, accepting them as contributory factors, to make every endeavor to overcome them.

Particularly in the field of the humanities the abstractor, if he is not the author himself, is likely to be a sympathetic volunteer in the field, rather than a full-time professional abstractor. This implies that he may well be a member of the teaching ranks of the profession (a situation that has occurred frequently in the long history of abstracting), engaged himself perhaps on some research of his own, but sufficiently public-spirited to devote some of his severely limited spare time to the task of conveying the work of some of his colleagues to the public at large by means of abstracts.

In many ways his is an ideal position, for his sympathy with the objectives of abstracts, and his interest in the subject-field, may result in the best form of abstract. Where he is too closely involved, being himself an expert in the very field of specialization that the author is dealing with, there is of course a danger that he could find it difficult to write a completely unbiased abstract, but the wise abstractor will in advance realize such dangers and suggest that it would be preferable that the abstract should be written by someone less committed and therefore more able to deal objectively with the work in hand.

PRINCIPLES, STANDARDS AND LENGTH

A good abstract is a coherent paragraph.

MLA ABSTRACT SYSTEM

An abstract is intended to convey all the original contribution to knowledge made by the original contributor—and nothing else. Thus an article may commence by summarizing the existing state of knowledge on a subject and what needs to be known; this has no place in an abstract. As the article proceeds it may, as part of its argument, draw on examples and similes derived from other people's work; these too will not be included in the abstract. The abstractor's task is simply to convey what the author himself has done, why he has done it, and by what steps he has arrived at his conclusions, together with these conclusions. Any other points are irrelevant.

It is important that the abstractor should use the vocabulary of the author as far as possible; paraphrase is dangerous and can lead the reader to channels of thought not intended by the author. Here of course the abstractor must use common sense, for not every author is a master of language or communication, and, being an expert in his own subject, he may employ a kind of telegraphic style that needs elucidation. Moreover he may use terms unfamiliar to the average reader—even in a specialized field—so the abstractor will need to add definitions of those terms where he deems it necessary. In abstracting from a foreign language, both paraphrase and interpretation may be necessary to a greater extent. Even the English used in different countries may have such subtle variations in meaning—*e.g.,* the difference in use of such quite ordinary terms as Institute, Review, Catalog(ue), etc.—that the abstractor will need to watch for and cope with these points.

It is also important that the abstractor follow exactly the same order of information as the author. This is necessary because any alteration in order may misrepresent the author's intention. Moreover, an alteration in order may make the reader's task more difficult when he attempts to identify the part of the original text dealing with the point that particularly interests him.

This raises an important issue. The author is dealing with a particular subject. The abstractor, too, is dealing with that subject. But the needs of users of abstracts are infinitely varied, and for every reader who is interested in the subject as a whole, there are many more readers who are interested in only one of its aspects (perhaps a fringe one) in the light of how it may affect their own interests. It is easy to overlook this very important aspect, and it is here that the editor of the abstract journal can step in to correct the approach of the abstractor who, working so closely with the material, tends to overlook the universal considerations and interests that govern the world of abstracts.

To convey the author's work adequately, it is necessary that the abstract should reflect just his degree of emphasis on any given point and no more. If the abstractor is interested in the subject and is sufficiently moved by the argument of a particular passage, he may tend to give an undue emphasis to that paragraph that will—to the reader of the abstract—convey more than the author intended. This is one of the many differences between a review and an abstract; though the reviewer may summarize the contents of a book, he may—because of his own interests or those of his reading public—devote much of his review to a few aspects on which he has specialized knowledge. Such an approach is totally unjustified in abstracting and the abstractor has at all times to beware of a natural tendency to confuse his own interests and lines of thought with those of the author.

Prejudice of course must not be allowed to affect an abstract in any way. Prejudice can arise from a thousand causes: the author's own reputation, his own attitude toward things, the largely unpopular nature of his line of approach, the unwelcome tenor of his conclusions, and so on. Similarly, no abstractor can be wholly free of bias—his strength is therefore in his awareness of his own prejudices and in his ability to overcome them in the interests of correct communication. Bias of any kind can ruin an abstract and therefore affect adversely the reputation of that particular abstracting service as a whole. Since bias can sometimes be unconscious, it is part of an editor's job to try to eliminate it wherever it may appear, his difficulty of course being to identify it as such.

The ultimate object of abstracting helps the abstractors and their editors to maintain a consistent policy. This object is to provide an easily-used analytical key to the advance of knowledge. This means that much will depend on the indexing of the abstracts. But the construction of adequate indexes can only be contrived if the abstracts contain the right information. If an author mentions a certain point that is not eventually included in the abstract, then it will not be included in the index to the abstract journal. Everything, in the first place, depends on the eternal vigilance of the editor of the journal; in the second place, on the careful work of the abstractor; and, in the third place, on the adequacy of the indexing process, which either is or shortly will be a largely mechanical operation. Abstracting is therefore teamwork of a high order, and any weakness in membership of that team will certainly be reflected in the degree of adequacy of the abstracts.

Much has been said and written about the desirable length of abstracts, and some formulae have been put forward concerning this point from time to time. However ingenious some of these have been, none has found general acceptance—and for a very good reason. The only criterion that can be laid down for the length of an abstract is that it should be long enough (and emphatically no longer) to convey adequately the author's concept. Thus, the knowledge in one article may be conveyed in an abstract only one-twentieth the size, while another article may need an abstract which is as much as a quarter of the size of the original. To invent, as the policies of some abstracting services have done, a Procrustean bed on which the overlong abstract is likely to suffer in the interests of uniformity or economy, is to court trouble. It is foolish to embark on an abstracting service unless it can be done adequately: any falling short of the ideal service tends to make users distrust the service as a whole.

There is one slight exception to the general policy concerning the length of abstracts. Where the original may be difficult to obtain, or where its language may be unfamiliar to most people, there is much to be said for providing a much more lengthy abstract in the interests of readers who may have to make do with that instead of being able to refer to the original. The advisability of a liberal policy of this nature needs no argument, but it affects the total volume of the abstracting operation to such a small extent, at the moment, that even questions of cost hardly arise.

APPROACH TO ABSTRACTING

> *Abstracting, as it exists today for the majority of the abstracts, includes a tremendous amount of redundancy.*
>
> JOHN JACOBS

Familiarity with the subject field of the abstracts is an essential. It cannot be sidestepped. The abstractor must be able to appreciate the significance of what the author has written for he is, in effect, pre-reading the author's contribution on behalf of the user of the abstract. The abstractor is the eyes and brain of the users of the material of the future: his object is to scrutinize the article in all the ways *they* would, and to record the points of interest that would strike them from all their different points of view. To do so, the abstractor must be knowledgeable about the subject on which the author is writing. He must be perceptive, so that he can extract the new contributions to knowledge the author is making from the mass of resumé of existing knowledge, example and illustration, that the writer has put forward in support of his theory.

But in addition the abstractor must be able to write a satisfactory abstract, and this is an increasingly difficult and specialized task. Thus it appears as though exceptional qualities are needed, in that the abstractor must not only be a subject-specialist but also a technician of a high order. This is, however, no more than is asked of a specialist librarian or information scientist, and in some ways a parallel can be drawn to the daily task of any member of the editorial staff of a technical journal. They too must be knowledgeable about the subject field, they must be able to sort the new from the established, and they must be able to write intelligently and intelligibly.

The editors of abstract journals issue instructions to their abstractors and these take many forms. But the gist is always the same: they ask for a clear and succinct single paragraph that conveys the author's intention, his scope and method, the results of his research and the inferences he draws.

This does not mean that the abstractor must write a kind of telegram in which the meaning is conveyed in a few key words to which the reader must himself add the connecting words that make the message readable. It has to be borne in mind that for the majority of readers the abstract is the full extent of the reader's exploration—he rarely proceeds to the full article, using instead the abstracts to keep himself up-to-date in the subject. In this connection it is well to remember that the greatest impact of the average article lasts no more than 3 years—after that time, its citation by other workers in the same field declines rapidly, indicating that the knowledge it conveys has been incorporated in books and that it is already partially superseded by later research. Therefore, the reader who mostly limits his reading to abstracts is only responding instinctively to the general tendency to regard all individual research items as milestones on the long road towards a horizon that constantly remains distant.

Ideally, the abstractor should read the article two or three times before embarking on his abstract. As experience is gained, this routine is often modified to suit individual circumstances, but it cannot be denied that the more familiar the abstractor is with the complete work, the more satisfactory his abstract is likely to be as a whole.

Having read the article the abstractor then proceeds to underline or make marginal notes of the passages whose import he feels must be incorporated in the abstract. This is work that has to be done with great care and deliberation since, once this process is completed, it is almost inevitable that the remainder of the article will be ignored, and the abstractor's attention will be concentrated on the marked passages.

The abstractor now has the task of constructing a narrative that conveys in brief all the information contained in these passages. Even nowadays, with all the experience and example to be found in the millions of abstracts already printed, it is not uncommon to find the new abstractor starting his abstract with words such as: "The author states ... ," or "This article concerns ...," or "This new contribution to ...." This kind of introduction is unnecessary and wasteful. Such introductions can be taken for granted. The abstractor's job is to launch immediately into the author's actual message:

> *Not*
> An attempt was made to
> construct an instrument ...

> *but*
> Attempted to construct
> an instrument ...

Much has been written about the tense and style of the abstract, and particular attention has been given to the advantages and disadvantages of using the active or the passive voice. There is also a tendency to advocate the use of the past tense, and here the justification seems incontestable since whatever is being described did in fact happen in the past. But even so, there should be no hard and fast rules on such points—what is far more important is the construction of an effective and satisfactory abstract, and questions of style and method should be elastic enough for the abstractor to be left plenty of room for maneuver. But *within* the abstract the tense should not change apart from exceptional circumstances. It is also important to avoid using the negative—this, in computer searching, could result in "false drops."

Having reduced each marked passage to an acceptable minimum, the abstractor now has the task of forming his sentences into a readable paragraph that conveys the spirit of the whole article without undue emphasis of one or more particular points. It is here that the abstractor's skill is fully called into play, for he usually cannot achieve this without modifying at least some of the sentences he has already written and, at this point, he finds it necessary to refer to the actual text and weigh the effect of his modifications on what has been written. If this process is not carried out thoroughly and with due reflection, the abstract is likely to be poor or indifferent, and thus the whole object of this expensive operation is impaired.

Not only must prejudice be avoided, but the abstractor is bound to avoid comment of his own. Should comment enter the abstract, then the result becomes a kind of review and not an abstract. Comment of any kind is out of place in an abstract, and should be reserved for other opportunities which the abstractor, since he is himself a specialist, can usually find without much difficulty.

Though the elimination of prejudice and opinion may not prove difficult to the abstractor, once he is familiar with his task, there remains the problem of misleading information. Where it is clear that the information given in the article is incorrect, the abstractor—as a specialist—naturally feels that this must be pointed out without delay. This can be done, where the misleading nature of the information is unmistakable to the reader, by inserting [sic] in square brackets immediately following the offending item, so that the reader of the abstract is warned to beware; e.g.:

> The United Kingdom's population in A.D. 2000 was estimated at 80,000 [sic] . . .

where, from the context, the figure of eighty million is clearly intended. No more is needed, for the readers of any abstracting service are mostly an expert audience quite as able to sort the good from the bad as the abstractor is, providing the latter has done his job properly in conveying the author's complete message.

And the conveyance of this message is best achieved as far as possible in the author's own words or vocabulary. Providing both author and abstractor are writing in the same language, there is no need for the latter to paraphrase the author's expressions or to substitute one word for another, except in the case of jargon that might not be understood by nonspecialists. Nevertheless, this quite often happens for the two protagonists have differing vocabularies, and the abstractor may well feel that he can do greater justice to the author's article by using a wider or more expressive vocabulary. As far as possible this temptation is to be resisted, since the abstractor's synonyms may sometimes turn out to be near-synonyms that could partly cloud the author's real meaning. In scientific and technological articles there is less of a danger of this happening than in those in the social sciences or humanities fields, but in either case, every endeavor should be made to use the writer's own words. The third person (even in the case of author-abstracts) should always be used.

It is essential to ensure that no important ideas in the original article are omitted in the abstract. At the same time, there is also the ever-present danger of failure to distinguish between major and minor items of information—an error which, if undetected, could misrepresent the document to the user of the abstract. Finally, the abstractor should not ordinarily include any information not given in the original document; if exceptional circumstances make this necessary, the additions should be clearly indicated. By keeping in mind at all times that the great majority of users have not seen and may never see the original article, the abstractor will find that his own product will improve in clarity and effectiveness.

AUTHORS AND TITLES

In abstracting, one does not miniaturize or summarize.
SOCIOLOGICAL ABSTRACTS: User's guide

The style in which the information concerning the authors and titles of works abstracted are presented has astonishing variations in current abstract journals. This is due to a series of individual house styles over which the abstractor has no control or influence, since it is unlikely that any abstract journal will change its style until some general agreement has been reached on a standard method of presentation. With the growing influence of computer compilation and indexing of abstracts, this may not be long distant, but for the moment the abstractor can but make himself familiar with the chief variations that are now in being and note the details and form of presentation that are required. Below is given a selection of examples of single author entry drawn from recent issues of well-known abstract journals, from which some idea of the range of variations that can be achieved will be gathered:

a. THE COUNSELING RELATIONSHIP AS A FUNCTION OF CLIENT-COUNSELOR PERSONALITY NEED AND SEX SIMILARITY

David J. Hebert, Ph.D.
Kent State University, 1967

Dissertation Abstracts, A, v.28 no. 11, May 1968, no. 4479-A

b. MACKINTOSH (J.P.)—**Scottish Nationalism**

International Political Science Abstracts, v. XVIII no. 1, 1968, p.75

c. MILLER, WILLIAM L. (William Beaumont Gen. Hosp., El Paso, Tex., USA.)

Sweat-gland Carcinoma: A Clinicopathologic Problem.

Biological Abstracts, v.49 no.13, 1st July 1968, no. 67893

d. ODELL, P.R. Economic integration and spatial patterns of economic development in Latin America.

Economic Abstracts, v.xvi no. 1, 1st June 1968, p.21

e. Podell, Lawrence (Dept. of Welfare of the City of New York, NY), OC-CUPATIONAL AND FAMILIAL ROLE-EXPECTATIONS.

Sociological Abstracts, vo.XVI, no.1, 1968, no. 9222

f. **van Praag, H.M.** (Psychiatric University Clinic, Groningen, Netherlands) **The Possible Significance of Cerebral Dopamine for Neurology and Psychiatry.**

Psychological Abstracts, v.42 no.5, May 1968, no. 6831

g. **Wagner, Edwin F.**
Continuity of Operator Functions.

Mathematical Reviews, v. 36 no. 1, July 1968

h. Williams, John R. (West Virginia U.). THE EMERGENCE OF THE LIB-ERAL PARTY OF AUSTRALIA.

Historical Abstracts, v.14 no.1 Mar. 68, no. 14:570

From these it will be noted that there is no general agreement on which is more worthy of emphasis, the author or the title. Only *Dissertation Abstracts* gives pride of place to the title, but *Historical Abstracts* and *Sociological Abstracts* signal the importance of the title by printing it in capitals, while *International Political Science Abstracts* counterbalances the influence obtained when setting the authors' names in capitals by printing the titles in bold face. *Mathematical Reviews* and *Psychological Abstracts* print both author and title in bold face, while *Biological Abstracts* and *Economic Abstracts* give the emphasis to the author's name by printing it in capitals, though the former evidently intends some counterbalance by underlining the title which, if it were printed, would have the result of setting the words in italics.

It will also be noted that even the presentation of the author's name has some small variations. Apart from *Dissertation Abstracts,* all the examples place the surname first, but *International Political Science Abstracts* puts the author's initials in parentheses. And there is clearly some disagreement concerning whether it is necessary to give the author's forenames in full—as can be seen by comparing the examples from *Historical Abstracts* and *Economic Abstracts.* It will further be observed that all but three of the journals give the name of the university or institution of which the author is a member. The curious will also notice that there are some interesting variations in the punctuation practice between author and title, and in the setting of one in relation to the other.

The following examples of multiple authorship, selected from the same issues of the same abstract journals, follow the same rules for setting, but have further variations in treatment:

a.   **Brown, Anne M., Stafford, Richard E., & Vandenberg, Steven G.** (U. Louisville School of Medicine) **Twins: Behavioral Differences.**

   Psychological Abstracts, v.42 no. 5, May 1968, no. 7065

b.   **Freedman, David; Purves, Roger**
      Timid Play is Optimal. II.

   Mathematical Reviews, v. 36 no. 1, July 1968

c.   JONES (G.W.) SMITH (B.C.), WISEMAN (H.V.)—**Regionalism and Parliament**

   International Political Science Abstracts, v. XVIII no. 1, 1968, p. 33

d.   Kristeller, Paul Oskar (Columbia U.), and Herman Michael Goldbrunner (German Hist. Inst., Rome). DER NACHLASS LUDWIG BERTALOTS: MIT EINEM VERZEICHNIS DER NACHGELASSENEN SCHRIFTEN.

   Historical Abstracts, v.14 no. 1, March 1968, no. 14.66

e.   MARSCHAK, TH., TH. K. GLENNAN and R. SUMMERS. Strategy for R. and D.: studies in the microeconomics of development.

   Economic Abstracts, v. xvi no. 1, 1st June 1968, p. 45

f.   REYNOLDS, E.H. (Nat. Hosp., London, Engl., U.K.), G. MILNER, D.M. MATTHEWS, and I. CHANARIN. Anticonvulsant Therapy, Megaloblastic Haemopoiesis and Folic Acid Metabolism.

   Biological Abstracts, v.49 no.13, 1st July 1968, no. 67748

g.   Weinberg, Martin S. & Elina Haavio-Mannila (Rutgers U, New Brunswick, NJ & U of Helsinki, Finland), THE MEDICAL PROFESSION IN FINLAND

   Sociological Abstracts, v. XVI no. 1, 1968, no. C9229

From these examples it will be noted that although the use of the comma to separate names is a fairly common feature, *Mathematical Reviews* uses a semi-colon for this purpose. Further, the word "and" is only used by three journals, and the symbol ampersand by two, the remaining two journals using neither. Even more interesting is the point that only *Psychological Abstracts, Mathematical Reviews* and *International Political cal Science Abstracts* reverse names after the first.

It will be appreciated that these remarkable variations in house style present some interesting problems for the computer programmers should they ever attempt to amalgamate or exploit abstract journals on a large scale, and that there is clearly a case for standardization as soon as possible. As has been said, the abstractor has no influence in this matter; he usually completes a standard form supplied by the abstract journal, in which the names and title are entered in a series of "boxes" from which the printer (or typist) sets up the abstract in the house style laid down for that journal.

BIBLIOGRAPHICAL REFERENCES

The abstracter must select the most pertinent material from the original.
SOCIOLOGICAL ABSTRACTS: User's Guide

The variety of ways in which details of author and title are given in abstract journals is easily exceeded by the number of variations in providing bibliographical references. While, as in the case of author or title details, the abstractor is powerless to influence or change the system, it may be said that the variations in making bibliographical references are due more in this case to the preference of the editor or committee responsible for publication of the abstracts. Once agreement has been reached on a suitable formula, this naturally becomes the house style for that journal, though not necessarily for that publishing house as a whole. The reasons for the variations are to be found in the history of each individual body responsible for issuing abstracts, and they reflect deep-rooted disagreements among scholars concerning what constitutes an effective bibliographical reference.

The following examples—more numerous than those that have been selected for author and title references, owing to the greater degree of variation now in force—give some idea of the different methods (all thought suitable by their individual editors) of conveying this essential information:

a.   **Ann. Hum. Genet.** (1965) 29, 127-138, (10 references, 7 figures)

   Statistical Theory and Method Abstracts, 9 (2), 1968, no. 413

b.   Zi, 1964, 29: 112-132

   Religious and Theological Abstracts VIII (1,2), Spring 65

c.   *Journal of Auditory Research,* 1967, **7** (2), 218

   Psychological Abstracts, 42 (5), May 1968, no. 7044

d. *Humanitas* [Mexico] 1961 2: 517-524
Historical Abstracts, 14 (1), March 1968, no. 635

e. Human Development, 1967, **10**, 128-131
Child Development Abstracts and Bibliography, 41 (5 & 6), Oct-Dec 1967, no. 751

f. *Austral. J. Exp. Biol. Med. Sci.*, 1966, **44**, 709-713
Nutrition Abstracts and Reviews, 37 (3), July 1967, no. 4446

g. *J. of Presbyterian Hist.* 1967 45 (4): 256-272
America: History and Life, 5(1), July 1968, no. 618

h. J PHYSIOL (London) 192 (3): 805-813. Illus. 1967.
Biological Abstracts, 49 (13), July 1, 1968, no. 67562

i. Social Work, 13 (1): 32-41, 1968
Abstracts for Social Workers, 4 (2), Summer 1968, no 394

j. *Ann. Math. Statist.* **38** (1967), 1273-1277
Mathematical Reviews, 36 (1), July 1968, no. 350

k. *Terra*, 79 (4), 1967, pp.113-120, fig, 3 tables, 21 refs.
Geographical Abstracts. D: Social Geography and Cartography, 1968/2, no/290

l. *Arch. Otolaryngol.*, 86, 1967, 639-644
dsh Abstracts, VIII (2), July 1968, no. 589

m. *BibSac* (498, '68) 139-146 [= Bibliotheca sacra]
New Testament Abstracts, 12 (3), Spring 1968, no. 968

n. *NaDoVySh* (FilNa), No. 4, 1967, 89-98 [= Nachnye doklady vysshei Shkoly (Filosofskie nauki)]
Soviet Periodical Abstracts, VII (4), February 1968, no. 788

o. *Amer. Polit. Sci. R.* 62 (1), March 1968: 88-109
International Political Science Abstracts, XVIII (1), 1968, no. 305

p. Int. Rev. missions, **54**, 215, July 1965, 343-52
African Abstracts, 19 (1), January 1968, no. 73

q. *Coll. and Res. Libr.*, **28** (6) November 1967, 416-422. References
Library Science Abstracts, 19 (1), 1968, no. 103

r.   *College and Research Libraries* **28** (3), 171-174 (1967 May). Tables

   Documentation Abstracts, 3 (1), March 1968, no. 317

s.   (The Quarterly journal of economics, Cambridge, no. 4, November, 1967, p. 628)

   [*NB* entry has previously stated number of pages]

   Economic Abstracts, XVI (1), June 1, 1968, no. P17

t.   *Economic Development & Cultural Change,* 1967, 15, 4, Jul, 398-407

   Sociological Abstracts, 16 (1), 15 February 1968, no. 09072

u.   The Teachers College Journal; v37 n1 p7, 32-39 Oct 1965

   Research in Education [ERIC], 4 (2), February 1969, ED 022 825

Of the twenty examples given above, it will be noted that only nine give the title of the periodical in full (although there is a very strong school of thought that maintains that all abbreviation of titles is inadvisable and a false economy). The remainder abbreviate the titles according to a variety of systems, most of them based no doubt on the principle of easy recognizability—at least, within a specialized audience. Emphasis of the title of the periodical, where this is thought necessary, is usually achieved by underlining or italicization, though *Statistical Theory and Method Abstracts* uses bold face for this purpose. Bold face is however used by no less than seven journals to indicate the volume number. It will also be observed that only one journal uses the ampersand symbol, the other printing "and" in full —even in *Library Science Abstracts* where abbreviations are used for all the other words in the title. Three journals give the city or country of publication, though in two cases this is clearly to distinguish the journals cited from others of the same name published elsewhere.

It is however in the details following the title of the periodical that the most remarkable variations occur. First of all, there is the question of the order of the bibliographical details given. The items to be arranged are:

   a) volume or number of issue of the periodical
   b) its date: day, month, year
   c) the inclusive page numbers of the article concerned

Of these, the year appears first in eight examples, and last in only three, so that in fully half the examples the year of publication must be sought in an intermediate position—of which the most that can be said is that this will always occur after the volume number, and that it will sometimes be set within parentheses. Only one journal, *New Testament Abstracts,* abbreviates the year. The month of issue, where quoted, is abbreviated in only one case out of five.

The volume and issue numbers are usually—but not always, for *Socio-logical Abstracts* is a notable exception—differentiated from each other by placing the issue number within parentheses.

Most surprising of all is the agreement to give inclusive page numbers in full. The apparent exception of *Economic Abstracts* is due simply to the fact that the number of pages of the article has been indicated earlier in the description. This unanimity exists despite the fact that it has been common practice for at least a century when setting page references in indexes to use a certain amount of abbreviation, *e.g.:*

                888-91   instead of   888-891
                24-6   24-26

This idea has failed to appeal to the editors of abstract journals, and their quest for a succinct setting has turned more to exploiting the possibilities of dropping punctuation symbols, and of using spaces instead. Careful examination of the examples given above will discover some very interesting and, in some cases, idiosyncratic uses of commas, parentheses, colons, etc., to distinguish one part of an entry from the next. It will also be noticed that a few journals helpfully add further details concerning the presence and size of bibliographies, maps, illustrations, tables, charts, etc., including an abbreviation in one case. The report number or contract information should of course always be stated in the bibliographical reference.

Here again is an incipient headache for the computer and its programmers in the future. The accurate coordination of these essential details in any large computer store could make for serious difficulties and produce long delays. The institution of some form of standardization as soon as possible is clearly advisable.

TYPES OF ABSTRACTS

Abstract preparation is a human task in today's environment. It can be expected to remain so for the forseeable future, because the promise of automatic abstracting has not yet been fulfilled.

SYSTEM DEVELOPMENT CORPORATION

Abstracts are either informative or indicative. One sometimes hears mention of a third variety, critical abstracts, and even of a fourth, telegraphic abstracts, but it is doubtful whether these types can be called true forms of abstract, since there is almost universal agreement that an abstract loses much of its value by being critical or telegraphic and, in any case, the former tends more to be a review rather than an abstract. Another phrase, "descriptive abstract," is a somewhat vague term that generally indicates the all-embracing category describing both informative and indicative abstracts, although it is sometimes used as an alternative for the term "indicative abstract." Thus, the classification of abstracts can be depicted as:

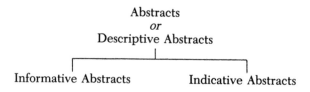

Abstracts
or
Descriptive Abstracts

Informative Abstracts   Indicative Abstracts

To complete the nomenclature of abstracts, mention must be made of three further terms: discipline-oriented abstracts; mission-oriented abstracts; and, "slanted abstracts." All three refer to abstracts in general. A discipline-oriented abstract is one that is written for an abstracting service dealing with a branch of knowledge, such as *Physics Abstracts* or *Biological Abstracts.* A mission-oriented abstract is one that is written for an abstracting service dealing with the applications of a branch of knowledge, such as *Railway Engineering Abstracts* or *Building Science Abstracts.* The

26

so-called "slanted abstract" is one that emphasizes only a subject-oriented portion of a document; it is chiefly used for the domestic needs of an organization, and can constitute a form of the mission-oriented abstract.

Informative and indicative abstracts perform different functions, and normally an article that lends itself to one form is usually not suitable for the other. The informative type of abstract has been compared to a leaf where all the flesh has been stripped away, leaving only a perfect structural skeleton, from which the leaf's original appearance can accurately be established. Ideally, the informative abstract is an intelligible and complete summary of the significant content and conclusions of the original article, so complete in itself that reference to the latter is not essential.

The same object cannot be achieved by the indicative abstract, which is a brief description written to help the user understand the scope of the original document, without giving him a detailed step-by-step account of the contents, *e.g.:*

> 1292. **Taeuber, Conrad. Invasion of Privacy. Eugenics Quarterly,** 1967, **14**(3), 243-246. - Reasons for Census Bureau data collection and methods to insure privacy are briefly described. - **S.G. Vandenberg.**
> *Psychological Abstracts,* vol. 42, no. 2, Feb. 1968, page 117

An informative abstract would have detailed the reasons and methods that are only mentioned here.

Both varieties of abstract are essential. Of the two, the informative abstract is the more important, the more popular, and the more used. It is suited to the vast majority of items that need to be abstracted. It is not, however, suitable for essays, for bibliographies, for surveys of research, for curriculum studies, for textbooks, for discursive or philosophic papers, for catalogues, or—for the most part—for symposia, *Festschriften,* or complete books. With regard to the last category, it must be emphasized that there are ways (described below) of dealing with their contents by means of informative abstracts. The type of document, if not indicated in the title, should be defined in the first sentence of the abstract—a point of especial importance when dealing with this type of material.

The informative abstract can, therefore, be divided into four sections; and the maintenance of this order—to which regular users of abstracts have become accustomed—is essential:

1) scope and purpose
2) methods employed and kind of treatment given
3) results obtained
4) conclusions, or the author's interpretation of the results

and the information given should be arranged in this order, though always within the limits of a single paragraph. Although an abstract should never be used as a primary source, it can sometimes effectively contribute to the clarity of the author's argument. What is equally important is that it can signal the existence of new data and new discoveries—items which the informative abstract will give in full (the *Referativnyi Zhurnal* even includes graphic and tabular material answering to this description). Since the readers of abstracts include many only generally acquainted with the subject-field who are inspecting them for useful material peripheral to their own subject-interests, the responsibility of the abstractor is increased since he has to keep in mind that his audience may partly comprise non-specialists. Thus the telegraphic phrases that might, at a pinch, be acceptable to users fully conversant with the subject, are unsuited to the wider audience, particularly when that audience almost certainly now includes readers from many foreign countries. It is also important for the abstractor to remember that even abstracts are more glanced at than read, so that not only the abstract as a whole but also each individual sentence needs to be free of any possibility of ambiguity, for the reader is entirely dependent on the abstractor's judgment and treatment.

The first of the four sections named above has particular importance. The busy reader, having read the title of the article may decide that the paper definitely is or is not of interest to him, or he may have sufficient doubt on this point that he needs further information before making a decision. Thus the description of the author's purpose or objectives can be conclusive in this respect. The reader is then dependent upon the remainder of the abstract for an accurate presentation of the author's intention. In the examples U, V and W (pp. 30-32), this is clearly established immediately, though the alternatives achieve this in different ways. As can be seen, the remainder of the texts of the abstracts, though essential, is of little use without this statement of intent. It is helpful to the reader to state the type of treatment: "brief," "exhaustive," "experimental," "theoretical," etc.

The second section, covering the methods or techniques employed, needs to be explicit. Unless *all* the details—including apparatus, equipment, and materials used—are given, the reader gets a partial, and therefore inaccurate, picture. Thus example V makes it clear that not only the actual process of marketing in the market-place is studied, but also other business systems. Again, one of the examples of W points out that such factors as availability of staff, parental attitudes, and the possibility of creating behavior problems among deaf teen-agers are evaluated.

The examples given have varying success in fulfilling the functions of the third and fourth sections, which are concerned with the author's results and conclusions. Comparison of the alternates is instructive in assessing how best to convey the author's findings—often not an easy task for the author who may have found that his questionnaires and fieldwork have failed to elicit unequivocal answers to the problems he has set out to resolve. In the case of new methods being employed in experimental results, their basic principles, range of operation, and degree of accuracy should be stated.

The fact that it is possible to compare different abstracts of the same article emphasizes the present position, that the interests of abstract journals in some cases overlap. Many periodicals and many articles remain without abstract treatment, while others are abstracted two or even three times. Although this may seem a wasteful duplication, from the point of view of the student of abstracts—and particularly from that of the would-be abstractor—the advantages of having comparative models are substantial. Careful comparison of treatment—especially if the text of the original document can also be studied—can be more instructive than pages of theory or of artificial examples shaped to the lecturer's ideas on the subject.

Examples X, Y and Z (pp. 33-35) illustrate the work of the indicative abstract. In the case of X, it is clearly impossible for the abstractor to deal with one hundred and fifty Swahili proverbs in any other way. In both the author's abstracts in example Y, neither gives exact details of the coverage and recency of the *Index Medicus,* or his reasons for saying that computers are not a solution for all bibliographical problems. In example Z, the general purport of the three articles is provided without much detail.

It is example Z that points most strongly to the way in which indicative and informative abstracts can combine to deal with such apparently intractable material as conference proceedings, symposia, *Festschriften,* and books. The indicative abstract can be employed to present a list of contents and an outline of general editorial policy under the entry for the complete work. The individual contents can then be treated separately by means of a series of informative abstracts, each placed under the specific subject-heading relevant to its theme. This method is more successful in the case of symposia and *Festschriften* than in the case of books, where the argument of one chapter may depend greatly on what has previously been established in other chapters. Nevertheless, the possibilities and advantages of this method are so great that they should always be examined—even if it is not possible to abstract every chapter, some of the most important can be so treated.

With regard to the abstracting of bibliographies, it is only possible to deal with them by means of the indicative abstract. Within these limits, however, much can be done. The bibliography naturally has a purpose, and its definition can be complemented by a summary of the principles by which individual items have been selected or rejected. This will involve a statement of the scope of the bibliography, the audience for whom it has been compiled, and the period of time covered. To these points should be added the approximate number of entries, and some indication of the system by which they are arranged. The existence of annotations and evaluations should be noted, and the provision of indexes and their nature are other points that should not be overlooked.

The abstracting of textbooks should include purpose; type of reader addressed; background knowledge assumed; a description of the general nature of the subject matter; and, any special methods employed, including details of illustrations, maps, recordings, audio-visual aids, or other auto-instructional materials.

U

555. KUPER, H. The Colonial Situation in Southern Africa. *J. modern Afr. Stud.,* **2,** 2, 1964, 149-64.

Distinctions may be made between those countries with and without a dominant white minority and on the basis of past and present contacts between Africans and Europeans. Various classifications have been worked out of people in both these groups. The structure of colonial society is outwardly rigid but there is in fact a considerable amount of mobility possible. Stereotypes and myths, held and believed by one group about the other, are common among Europeans and Africans.

R. Mansell Prothero

African Abstracts/Bulletin analytique africaniste, vol. 16, no. 4, Oct. 1965, page 150

14. 1462   KUPER (H.) - **The colonial situation in Southern Africa.** *J. mod. Afr. Stud.* 2 (2), July 64: 149-164.

Salient structural and ideological similarities found throughout Southern Africa validate analysis in terms of a "colonial situation." Each of the countries (the Republic of South Africa, Southern Rhodesia, Northern Rhodesia, Nyasaland, Swaziland, Bechuanaland, Basutoland, Mozambique and Angola) has its specific history of external contact and internal adjustment, but in all a basic cleavage exists along arbitrarily defined characteristics of "race" and "civilization." This classification affects the major institutions of the society and produces institutional pluralism and opposed values. At the same time, colonialism itself induces and may perpetuate a series of cross-cutting interests and secondary conflicts within the major segments. The complex divisions in these societies are expressed in mutually derogatory stereotypes, and rationalized by a growing mythology. Economic innovations *per se* create new divisions and do not resolve the structural and ideological conflicts. [A]

International Political Science Abstracts/Documentation politique internationale vol. XIV, no. 4, 1964, page 574

V

C2091   Neale, Walter C., Harpal Singh, & Jai Pal Singh (U of Texas, Austin, Punjab Agri'al U, India, Gov'al Coll, Sardarshahr, Rajasthan, India), KURALI MARKET: A REPORT ON THE ECONOMIC GEOGRAPHY OF MARKETING IN NORTHERN PUNJAB, *Econ. Develop. Cult. Change,* 1965, 13, 2, Jan, 129-168

A report of the results of an investigation into the structure of marketing in a market town in northern Punjab, and into the pattern of arrivals and prices of farm produce, from Oct. 1960 to Apr. 1961. The survey focused on a description of the appearance, morphology, and procedures of an Indian farm market. In addition to the market places, data is presented on other businesses, the livestock fair, payment and finance, the farmer and his agent, the cooperative marketing society, storage facilities, the problems of interpreting prices, and measures of within-month price variation. The growth and pattern of business of the market is detailed re seasonal pattern of marketing and seasonal variations in price, 1959 to early 1961. 8 maps. E. Weiman.

Sociological Abstracts, 14(6), Sept. 1966, page 755

66C/49 Kurali market. A report on the economic geography of marketing in northern Punjab. W.C. NEALE, *Economic Development and Cultural Change,* Chicago, 13(2), 1965, pp. 129-168, 15 figs, 4 tables, 2 refs.

In 1960/61 the marketing structures of Kurali, N. Punjab, and the pattern of arrivals and prices of farm products were investigated. The main aspects covered were: 1) the appearance, morphology and procedures of an Indian farm market, and 2) factual discoveries which appeared to disprove accepted theories. Since insufficient data were available, the investigation was based mainly on the development and mapping of indices of market intensities. Research was devoted to the main products (food grains, groundnuts, gur and Shukr) while the livestock and vegetable markets were only touched upon. The Kurali market differs from more organized markets only in the uncertainty resulting partly from wide variations in daily deliveries and orders, partly from a great reluctance to divulge information which might be made available. Another element of unpredictability is the lack of standard grades for products. Divergencies from the hypothetical pattern of concentricity were due largely to topography and natural conditions and less to the inadequate road network and competition of other markets. Interviews held were quite haphazard, but still added to the overall picture. In general, the farmer does not seem to be so badly off in the market as would appear from the literature on the subject. Farmers can withhold food produce from the market and are not so weak financially as they were in relation to the arthiyas (farm produce merchants).
- H.K. from W.A.E.R.S.A. 7(2), no. 761

Geographical Abstracts C: Economic Geography, 1966/1, pages 18-19

W

10458. **Craig, William N., & Anderson, Peter E.** (U. Pittsburgh) **The Role of Residential Schools in Preparing Deaf Teen-agers for Marriage.** *American*

Annals of the Deaf, 1966, **111**(3), 488-498. -Responses to 60 of 66 questionnaires sent out to public residential school administrators are summarized with respect to whether the schools permitted dating and social activities among their pupils and/or provided programs incorporating such training opportunities. There was "much higher agreement by the administrators on provisions for dating and social relationships than on family life education." About 1/4 of the administrators were uncertain about parental attitudes toward such social activity and 1/3 were uncertain about parental attitudes toward sex education in the school. -T.E. Newland.

Psychological Abstracts, volume 40, no. 9, September 1966, page 982

192. CRAIG, William N. (U. Pittsburgh, Pa.), & ANDERSON, PETER E. **The Role of Residential Schools in Preparing Deaf Teen-agers for Marriage.** *American Annals of the Deaf,* 1966, 3, 488-498.

This study was designed to determine how the residential schools for the deaf are meeting the problem of preparing deaf teen-agers for marriage. A questionnaire on preparing teen-agers for marriage was sent to the administrators of 66 residential schools for the deaf. Returns from 92% of these schools were examined to determine how the schools approached the dating and social relationship area and provided for family life education. The role of the residential school for the deaf in preparing teen-agers for marriage appears to rest upon the administrators' assessment of the need for such a program. Such factors as availability of staff, parental attitudes, and the possibility of creating behavior problems among the teen-agers are evaluated. Differences of opinion, as expressed by the administrators, appear to be based on positive feelings rather than on casual concern. - Authors' Summary.

Child Development Abstracts and Bibliography, volume 42, nos. 1&2, Feb.-Apr. 1968, page 45

155. CRAIG, W.N. (U. Pittsburgh, Pa.) and ANDERSON, P.E. The Role of Residential Schools in Preparing Deaf Teen-agers for Marriage. *Amer. Ann. Deaf,* 111, 1966, 488-498.

60 public residential schools for the deaf responded to a two-part questionnaire dealing with (a) policies on dating and social activities and (b) family life education. Most administrators felt that a school should provide social activities for its teen-age students. Responses indicated variation in the approach to family life education. Most schools taught homemaking. Half of the schools made formal provisions for sex education. A third were unsure of parental attitudes toward sex education. - *B.W. Rosenbloom*

dsh Abstracts, volume VII, no. 1, Jan. 1967, page 34

X

604. KNAPPERT, Jan. "Rhyming Swahili Proverbs." *Afrika u. Uebersee,* 49, 1, 1966, 59-68.

The wealth of proverbs in Swahili is a product of the long traditions of the Swahili themselves and the contributions made by people of other tribes who have settled in Swahili-speaking towns. The rhyming proverbs here presented were collected by the author in Mombasa in 1962 and in N.E. Tanganyika in 1963.   *A. Vorbichler*

African Abstracts, vol. 18, no. 3, July 1967, page 125

AFRIKA UND ÜBERSEE [Africa and Overseas] (Hamburg, Germany), XLIX: 1, June, 1966. 7. Knappert, Jan. "Rhyming Swahili Proverbs," pp. 59-68.

Briefly annotated presentation of 150 Swahili rhyming proverbs collected by the author in Mombasa and Northeast Tanganyika in 1962-63. (Swahili text and English translation)   - William Templer

Abstracts of Folklore Studies, vol. V, no. 1, Spring 1967, page 6

Y

Some Proposals for Handling the Information Problem—A Brief Bibliographical Essay   Carrol H. Quenzel

Computers are not a solution for all bibliographic problems. Nevertheless, more machine control of information in university and other research libraries seems inevitable because of the frequent necessity and difficulty of determining what, if any, research has been done on certain subjects.

The Library of Congress is currently conducting a computer feasibility study. The use of a Listomatic camera has increased the coverage and recency of *The Index Medicus.* One midwestern library is so pleased with the results of a preliminary study that it is planning to convert to an automated operation soon.

A radical reorganization of university and research libraries is envisioned by some writers. One proposal calls for a national research library from which copies of desired items could be obtained by dialing the appropriate number. Others would have this service provided by six regional core libraries.

Certain writers stress thorough investigation and extensive planning before any library decides to automate. Two of these specialists question the existence of a general information inundation.

Author's summary given at the head of his article - *American Documentation,* vol. 14, no. 2, April 1963, page 145

13812   Some Proposals for Handling the Information Problem—A Brief Bibliographical Essay. Carrol H. Quenzel. *Amer. Doc.,* **14** (2) April 1963, 145-148. References.

Computers are not a solution for all bibliographic problems, but more machine control of information in university and other research libraries seems inevitable and the Library of Congress is currently conducting a computer feasibility study. Certain writers stress thorough investigation before any library decides to automate.   (Author)

Z

2968   Russian Abstracting and Special Library Work
W.G. Cass
Librarian, **42** (4) April 1953, 69-71

A review of the three articles on problems in the organization of information services, especially in abstracting and technical library work, which have appeared in the organ of the Academy of Sciences, *Vestnik Akad Nauk SSSR,* 1952, **22** (8,9), 41-45, 46-55, 82-91. The first article deals with the State Scientific Library (3-1/2m. books and journals) and its services, the second is on the mechanization of information work and abstracting. The third discusses the general principles and problems of abstracting; an account is given of abstracting in the West and in Russia and the essential requirements of an efficient abstracting service are discussed—scope, critical function, type of reader classification.
[Also in *Lib. World,* **54** (636) June 1953, 207-209]   G.P.S.

Library Science Abstracts, vol. IV, no. 3, 1953, page 159

2855   Abstracting and Library Work in the USSR
W.G. Cass
Nature, **171** (4352) 28 March 1953, 555-557.

Summarises three articles that have recently appeared in the *Vestnik Akad. Nauk.* The first describes the work of the State Scientific Library, which gives special consideration to enquiries from students, but also makes its services available through 260 industrial centres. Fifty specialists and an editorial staff prepare abstracts, which are usually issued as single leaflets. The second discusses mechanical aids, giving some principles but no examples. The third deals with abstracts, which must be distinguished from annotations and reviews. A summary should be given with the article. Several Soviet abstract publications are noted, though the original 1928 scheme was too grandiose to be properly realized. An abstract service should be established on a uniform plan, based on a logical classification of the whole field of knowledge, of which the main classes are indicated, and having where possible a single journal for a main subject.   D.J.F.

Library Science Abstracts, vol. IV, no. 2, 1953, pages 122-123

EDITING

*Abstracts rarely give the exact informa-
tion the reader wants to know.*

MARIAN P. ANDERSON

The editing of abstracts is work of the greatest importance. Consistency is essential, and only the editor can visualize the contents of his journal as a whole and fully appreciate the necessity for a policy that enables his readers to understand and evaluate the journal's contents accurately. The work is arduous and unremitting and demands incessant attention to matters of minute detail. For example, it is essential to keep constantly in mind that the readership of any abstract journal nowadays is certain to be international, and therefore the language of its abstracts must be clear and incapable of misinterpretation by readers who have a limited acquaintance with the language of the abstracts. The editor's routine is similarly exacting. In the first place, it is necessary to keep to a rigorous time schedule. If the journal is to be effective it must be published regularly and the time-gap between the publication of the original articles and the resultant abstracts kept to a minimum. Since much of the work of abstracting is either voluntary or only rewarded by a small honorarium, this is not easy to achieve or maintain. While the contributor may never be lacking in good will or enthusiasm, too often his work of abstracting is a sparetime hobby or occupation to which he can devote only a small amount of time.

Thus, it is the editor's province to maintain exact records of what has been undertaken, what has been completed, and what is still outstanding. Therefore, the editor must have an efficient "suspense" system of reminders that neither alienates the contributor nor lulls him into a false feeling that no particular hurry is required. Moreover, the unexpected must be provided for: sudden absences, resignations or illnesses of contributors— all must be covered and reserves built up to cope with any lapses, and new contributors must regularly be recruited, trained and encouraged by allocation of at least small amounts of work so that they are ready to play their full part at the right moment.

Abstracts must be uniform in content, style, and presentation. In many cases the contributor is asked to use a standard form, supplied by the journal and designed for its special needs, on which he writes or types his abstract. These forms, which vary considerably in design, all include the following allocations of space:

a) bibliographical references
b) text of abstract
c) further information

The space for bibliographical references is usually divided into a number of boxes that break up the references into details—author's surname, author's initials or full forenames, title of article, translation of the title if in a foreign language, etc.—so that the entry for publication can be set up without difficulty. Precise details of punctuation are not involved, since these will be dealt with by the printer or editor according to the house style of that particular journal.

The space for the text of the abstract is the largest part of the form, and here the abstractor has free play. Thus, his entry, while commonly in typescript may, in some circumstances, be handwritten and, in either case, it may contain misspellings or words that are not easy to read, deletions, overtypings, omissions or apparent omissions. Wherever possible these must be compared with the text of the original article and corrected if necessary. In some cases it may be important to check back one or two items with the abstractor, a process that can occasion heavy delays at times.

The style of the abstract may be responsible for more difficulty. The instructions given to abstractors are usually explicit, and sometimes quite verbose, but abstractors are only human and they may choose to ignore instructions from time to time. The commonest fault is the repetition of information in the title. Another understandable mistake is to commence the abstract with such words as "This study sets out to prove . . . ," or "This article is the result of . . ."—words unnecessary in the world of abstracting. These typical beginner's faults are usually eliminated early, though they tend to reappear from time to time. Every editor is in any case well aware that on the stylistic effectiveness of the first sentence often depends the likelihood of the user's continuing to read the remainder of the abstract —and an unread abstract is a useless abstract!

Faults in style are frequently more subtle. An abstractor may write:

"A survey conducted in 1970 by the American Library Association . . ."

a phrase which the editor will probably compress and improve to read:

"An American Library Association survey in 1970 . . ."

Or, the abstractor may write:

"This is an anthology of autobiographical notes . . ."

The editor would delete "This is" since those two words are clearly unnecessary in an abstract. Again, the contributor may say:

"Stylistic resemblances are apparent in a number of passages in the poems . . ."

whereas the editor may prefer:

"A number of passages in the poems show stylistic resemblances . . ."

Or, the abstractor may write:

"In an effort to combat illiteracy in the Gold Coast, a plan for mass education was undertaken . . ."

for which the editor may substitute:

"A mass education plan for the Gold Coast attempted to combat illiteracy . . ."

In most cases editorial revision reduces the number of words used, but this is not the chief aim of the editor who is far more interested in achieving an effective way of conveying the information contained in the original article without including one unnecessary word or phrase.

Contributors are therefore encouraged to type their entries double-spaced to enable the editor to make alterations without too much difficulty, although in some cases retyping becomes necessary. Since speed is essential throughout the editorial process, it is rarely possible for the editor to refer alterations to the contributor for approval, and it must be assumed that abstractors infrequently have time to compare their original efforts with the finished product, since they continue their invaluable work without overmuch protest—or that they have come to rely on the editorial staff to deal with any small lapses, or that they at least appreciate the need for a strong editorial control in the interests of maintaining a high standard of product. Some editors courteously make it a practice to send a copy of the edited script of the abstract in its final form to the abstractor and this is an indirect but most effective training system.

There should be a space provided on the abstract form to include further details such as the number of references cited by the author. It may also include the contributor's recommendations for indexing entries. A good abstractor may not always be a good indexer, and the editor's indexing staff is therefore obliged to scrutinize these recommendations very closely. The contributor naturally sees things from the point of view of the individual article which he has just abstracted; the indexers' viewpoint is that deriving from their duty to provide an index to many articles which must subsequently be combined with several similar indexes to form a satisfactory annual—and even a multi-annual—index. Thus the overall vision of the indexers can frequently be in conflict with the contributor's suggestions, and the latter must therefore be modified or expanded or completely altered to serve the needs of the great variety of potential users and give them the index entries which their very varied standpoints severally require. Where, of course, the journal uses an agreed thesaurus of index terms, the indexing must be left entirely to the editorial staff if —as in these days of computer-storage—it is impossible to furnish copies of the thesaurus to the individual contributors.

It is increasingly an editorial practice to incorporate relevant abstracts published in other abstracting journals; such mutual exchange arrangements enable editors to avoid duplication of work. The use of author-abstracts printed at the head of the original article also saves time. With regard to the latter, editing may be necessary because the author may have referred to charts, tables, etc., in the text.

Abstractors are not always asked for suggestions concerning the classification of their abstracts, although the contents of most abstract journals are classified. Thus the journal's classifiers must usually assign the classification symbols themselves—a task that most often requires scrutiny of the original article. The more detailed the classification system used by the journal, the more exacting this task may be. And, finally, both indexers and classifiers must provide for cross-references where necessary. They are both in fact working under a basic set of rules built upon experience and a series of commonsense precedents.

Each abstract must also be provided with a unique reference—usually a serial number—which identifies it and differentiates it from all other abstracts. Unless this is done accurately confusion can occur at a later stage which may be difficult to resolve. Since this reference will usually depend on the abstract's classified position in the appropriate part of the journal, it cannot be awarded until the contents have been correctly assembled ready for publication. On this reference will depend the index entries and also the cross-references in the body of the journal; therefore iron control of this essential feature is imperative. Serial numbers must also be given to those items which, owing to the nature of their contents are listed (for the sake of comprehensive coverage) without abstracts or, at best, with some such note as "The title describes the document," or "Listed for reference only."

Most abstract journals attempt to maintain roughly the same size of issue throughout the year, and to achieve this there must be a deadline so that, when enough abstracts have been assembled, new items are automatically deferred until the next issue. Good teamwork between abstractors and the editorial staff is thus of the highest importance, and it is much to the credit of the editors that this appears to be present in almost every case.

The editorial routine at the Excerpta Medica Foundation throws valuable light on what is involved in large-scale abstracting. Each year some twenty thousand copies of periodicals from all parts of the world are received and duly registered at the Foundation's headquarters in Amsterdam. The periodicals' complete contents are then microfilmed. A team of medical Assignment Editors, after scrutinizing the journals, allocates each article to the appropriate specialist Executive Editor, since the Foundation publishes thirty-four English language abstracting journals. Articles having interdisciplinary aspects are specially considered, and abstracts of their contents may appear in several of the abstract journals. To ensure that items can be retrieved immediately, bibliographical data, one to five classification categories, primary and secondary indexing terms, and any other essential items of information are all punched on paper tape and fed into the computer. Machine searches on highly specific topics can be conducted within four to six weeks of receipt of the original document. The computer, at this stage, puts out an Abstract Form containing all this data, and the Executive Editor considers this information, together with the original article, for decision as to whether it is to be abstracted for publication *and* for data bank storage. Those articles that are approved for publication are then sent to the appropriate specialist abstractors who are qualified for this task both professionally and linguistically. There is an international roster of over four thousand abstractors, and many of the abstracts are prepared in foreign languages and then translated into English by members of the Foundation's Translations Department. The translated texts are checked for scientific and linguistic accuracy by a group of Medical Styling Editors. After final editing and specialist checking, the text of the abstract is punched on paper tape and brought together with other data relevant to the original article which was previously fed into the data bank. About two hundred thousand citations of articles are stored annually, and about one hundred and forty thousand abstracts are published in the Foundation's journals.

At the other end of the scale there is the small abstract journal produced by an organization for internal use only. Here production may take a very modest form, but the same high standards of editing are as necessary as in those issued for general circulation, for any relaxation may result in mistrust and misinformation, and thus impair the company's efficiency. In this connection, questions of security arise also. For example, information concerning proprietary or similar matters may be given which needs to be restricted to approved personnel. Documents having a high security classification may be included. The editor must then choose between constructing an abstract of the same classification, which will require that the whole of that issue of the journal be of the same classification, or including a more general and less informative abstract which need not be classified. There is no general agreement on which method is preferable, but it is clear that every document should be covered by some form of entry, so that at least its existence is not overlooked. This is necessary since the security classification of any document will be reduced or removed sooner or later.

INDEXING

*The abstract was described as a method
devised several centuries ago to cope
with excessive publication. It is no
longer able to cope . . . .*

MARY L. TOMPKINS

To exploit abstracts fully, their indexing needs to be of a very high standard. Clearly, there must be entries for all authors and for all personal and other proper names mentioned in the abstracts, but these constitute only one of the several ingredients, and certainly not the most important. The real emphasis of abstracts is on the detailed analysis of subject matter, and in the effective indexing of abstracts data. The editors of abstracting journals have displayed much ingenuity in planning how these goals are to be achieved.

But, first of all, it is necessary to consider what items constitute the main types of index because, with some exceptions, abstract journals tend to provide not one inclusive index but rather several different indexes, each devoted to a single aspect. These can comprise a combined comprehensive index such as that used by *Historical Abstracts* as shown here:

INDEX
HISTORICAL ABSTRACTS
VOLUME 16   NUMBER 2/3   (Abstracts 16:1007-2912)

COMBINED INDEX OF AUTHOR, BIOGRAPHICAL, GEOGRAPHICAL, AND SUBJECT ENTRIES

NOTE:

* BIOGRAPHICAL ENTRIES (Names followed by an asterisk)   ** AUTOBIOGRAPHICAL ENTRIES (Names followed by two asterisks)

Personal names without asterisks are authors of articles. Names of abstracters are not listed in the Index.

A

Aagaard, K., 1478
Abad Pérez, Antolín, 1582, 1681, 1682
Abadal y Vinyals, Ramón de*, 1021

Present Names
Customs, 1523
Exploration and Discovery, 1519
Foreign Policy
France, 1139
Great Britain, 1139

Agnelli, Giovanni*, 2244
Agramonte, Roberto, 1741
Agrarian Movements and Uprisings See 'Agricultural Labor'
Agrarian Party (Bohemia), 2613
Agrarian Party (Bulgaria), 2598

Russian Empire (to 1918), 2833, 2834
Spain, 1442
Turkey (from 1918), 2815
USSR (since 1918), 2882, 2891, 2897
Venézuela, 1966

41

HISTORICAL ABSTRACTS (CONTINUED)

Other types of index include:

1) Names of authors, editors, translators, reviewers, and other personal names mentioned.
2) Titles of periodicals abstracted.
3) References to quotations of important texts.
4) Bibliographical citations of other works (citation indexes).
5) Book reviews.
6) Abstractors.
7) Special indexes—ethnic, linguistic, statistical, geographical, etc.
8) Subject index to the classification used in the abstract journal.
9) All abbreviations used in the abstract journal.
10) Institutions.
11) Analytical subject index to abstracts.
12) Continuity index.
13) Keyword title index.

No abstract journal includes all of these types of index, but one, *New Testament Abstracts,* provides six of them, and *Statistical Theory and Method Abstracts* offers five plus an "analysis of secondary classifications" as shown here:

ANALYSIS OF SECONDARY CLASSIFICATIONS

VOL. 9: No. 1 (1-264)

In order to assist subscribers to make the fullest use of the abstracts, the quarterly analysis will show how each secondary classification is associated with any primary classification. By this means a full reference background can be obtained for a statistical technique falling within any part of the classification scheme.

SECONDARY CLASSIFICATION	PRIMARY CLASSIFICATION AND ABSTRACT NUMBER
0.0	0.10, 11; 9.1, 186
0.1	10.4, 199
0.2	6.5, 145
0.6	0.10, 12; 0.1, 15
0.7	9.1, 183
0.8	5.0, 131
0.9	9.1, 187
0.10	1.1, 30; 1.5, 44; 9.1, 185; 10.0, 194
1.0	1.5, 49
1.1	2.10, 61; 4.3, 109
1.2	1.5, 31; 4.3, 99
1.3	0.6, 14
1.5	1.3, 18; 1.3, 19; 1.0, 34;

Even within these groupings there are some interesting variations:

1) *Name indexes.* The practice of including all personal and corporate names cited in the title, abstract, bibliographical references, etc., is almost universal, though there are the usual variants that occur in name indexes the world over. These relate mainly to details in punctuation. Thus a name such as A. Smith may appear in different form in different indexes:

> Smith, A
> Smith, A.
> Smith (A)

with varying ideas on whether the surname should be shown in capitals throughout, or in upper and lower case. Only full names will help users differentiate between two people of the same surname and initial, but the rigid practice of some abstracting services prevents their meeting this difficulty. The unhappy tendency to set the name index in small type is unfortunately too general to overlook and such indexes are unnecessarily difficult to consult. This practice usually occurs where the index is a photographically reduced image of an original typescript or computer printout.

2) *Indexes of titles of periodicals.* This form of index usually comprises the full title of the journal and the abbreviation (not always standard) of the title used in the abstract journal. In many cases the abbreviation is given first. In some cases additional and very useful information, such as the volume number and issue number and date of the periodical actually abstracted in that issue of the journal, is cited; and one or two journals add references to the numbers of the abstracts relating to the periodical concerned. Some journals include place of publication of the periodical, most do if there can be any doubt as to which of two journals with similar titles is intended. At least one journal, *New Testament Abstracts,* asterisks periodicals recently added to their list as shown here:

LIST OF JOURNALS (Continued)

Freiburger Zeitschrift für Philosophie und Theologie (Fribourg)
Furrow (Maynooth)
Geist und Leben (Würzburg)
Gnomon (Munich)
Gordon Review (Beverly Farms, Mass.)
Greek Orthodox Theological Review (Brookline, Mass.)
Gregorianum (Rome)

Laval Théologique et Philosophique (Quebec)
*Living Light (Washington, D.C.)
London Quarterly and Holborn Review (London)
Lumen Vitae (Brussels)
Lumière et Vie (St. Alban-Leysse)
Lutheran Quarterly (Gettysburg, Pa.)
Lutherische Rundschau (Stuttgart)
Maison-Dieu (Paris)

3) *Index of text references.* This occurs only where most abstracts relate to an established text. An example of this is the Bible. Both *New Testament Abstracts* and *Religious and Theological Abstracts* provide special indexes of scriptural references (chapter and verse are given wherever possible) arranged in the generally accepted order of the scriptures. The special indexes may include some references not fully identified in the abstract itself.
a.   Special Index (sample) from *New Testament Abstracts*
b.   Special Index (sample) from *Religious and Theological Abstracts*

a.

INDEX OF PRINCIPAL SCRIPTURE TEXTS

The numbers following the scriptural texts refer to entries, not pages.

Matthew	142–146,	27:45-46	881	5:33-39	177–178r,
	548–550, 859r	27:46	882		195
1–2	551r, 860–861	27:51	168	5:34	563
1:25	147	28:16-20	169, 560	6:17	149
2	862			7:21	196
2:11	552	Mark	170r–175,	7:24-25	871
3:11	863		561, 883–886	8:4-15	158, 872
3:13-17	103	1:16-18	562	8:4-18	555, 873

INDEX OF PRINCIPAL SCRIPTURE TEXTS (CONTINUED)

b.

4) *Index of bibliographical citations* (citation index).

BIBLIOGRAPHIC PAPERS

The following index gives a representation of all papers, abstracted in volume nine, where the number of references exceeds 20.

0. Mathematical Methods	No.	refs.		6. Relationships— continued			
Rényi	9/11	0.10	24	Walker & Duncan	9/155	6.8	24
Wold	9/16	0.1	25	Henshaw	9/411	6.1	25
Dieter	9/559	0.8	24	Anscombe	9/719	6.1	45
Tan	9/575	0.8	65	Cattell	9/725	6.3	54
Benedetti	9/873	0.4	29	Cattell	9/726	6.3	30
Dwyer	9/877	0.6	21	Rao	9/744	6.3	37
Künzi	9/882	0.8	28	Williams	9/745	6.4	44

5) *Index of book reviews.* This form of index, together with (4), usually relates to citations in the text of abstracts of other works to which attention has been drawn. Citation indexes have earned increasing interest during the past few years, and it is noticeable that while references to periodical articles grow markedly less after the first five years of publication, references to much older

established books (sometimes in new editions) continue over a very much longer period of time.

INDEX OF BOOK REVIEWS

Aland, *Studien zur Überlieferung des Neuen Testaments und seines Textes*, 49r, 387r.
Apocalypse de Baruch, 1015r.
Baarda, *De Betrouwbaarheid van de Evangeliën*, 78r.
Barrett, *A Commentary on the First Epistle to the Corinthians*, 260r, 593r–594r, 937r.
————, *Jesus and the Gospel Tradition*, 93r.
Beardslee, *Literary Criticism of the New Testament*, 744r.
Beumer, *Die Inspiration der Heiligen Schrift*, 2r.
Bjerkelund, *Parakalô*, 231r, 570r.

New Testament Abstracts

6) *Index of abstractors.* This usually provides a key to the initials (where they are used instead of the full name) appended to an abstract, though some journals also give some detail concerning the institution each abstractor represents. Order is sometimes by initials, sometimes by full name.

7) *Special indexes.* Some abstracts require special indexes owing to the nature of their subject matter. Thus *Statistical Theory and Method Abstracts* includes an index of new statistical tables, but these do not cover tables presenting data on results of an investigation. *African Abstracts/Bulletin analytique africaniste* provides an ethnic and linguistic index. *Economic Abstracts* and *Geographical Abstracts* include a geographical index.

a.   Geographical index (sample). *Economic Abstracts.*

ETHNIC AND LINGUISTIC INDEX

NOTE: Entries are under first letter of stem and prefixes such as Ba-, Ki- in Bantu languages are generally omitted.

Abenyubi 441	677, 682, 712 (Urbantu),	Dinka 64, 304, 657-8
Abua 353	745, 871, 892, 900, 911-13	Djem 626
Acholi 64, 216, 657-8	Bantu-Guinean 364, 526	Dodos 894
Adangme 105	Baraguyu 881	Dogon 90, 113, 481, 528, 802
Adansi 558	Bari 64, 657-8	Dormaa 542
Adyukru **77, 783**	Basque 526, 733	Duala 389
Afa (Pa'a) 337	Baule, Bauli 521, 547, 781	Dyalonke (Djalonke) 603
Afar 496-8, 760-1, 766	Baya 863	Dyola (Diola) 848
Afro-Asiatic 749	Bemba 447	Dyula 542
Agaw 749	Bembe 391, 628	

b.   Geographical index (sample). *Geographical Abstracts.*

REGIONAL INDEX 1968/C Nos. 1-6

WORLD − General
9, 49, 79-81, 90-2, 112, 134, 145-6, 149-51, 174-5, 211, 230, 261, 336, 353, 359, 447, 463, 533-5, 554, 574-5, 582, 622, 645, 654-6, 666, 669, 683, 707, 730, 775, 822, 824, 851, 859-60, 940, 1015-6, 1052-3, 1153-4, 1205, 1222, 1284, 1394, 1435, 1460-1, 1522, 1528, 1564-5, 1583, 1627.

REGIONAL INDEX (CONTINUED)

EUROPE — General
93-4, 152-3, 254-5, 286, 361, 826, 904, 941, 1056, 1061, 1285, 1316,
1458, 1607, 1613.
WESTERN EUROPE — General
192-6, 222, 231, 285, 291, 392, 440, 449, 488-91, 540-1, 558, 687-8, 712-3,
761-3, 781-2, 903, 993, 1017, 1021, 1063-4, 1184, 1315, 1366-8, 1395,
1397-8, 1523, 1566, 1608, 1652, 1655.
Great Britain & Ireland
20, 34-5, 37, 50, 57, 223, 278, 290, 306, 362-3, 383-4, 420-4, 514, 586,
591, 597, 607-9, 619, 630-1, 646-7, 657-8, 670, 708-9, 866, 942, 946, 950,
990-2, 1014, 1017, 1075, 1113, 1156-9, 1286, 1317, 1399, 1400, 1414-5,
1428-9, 1453-5, 1462, 1482-3, 1491, 1529, 1537, 1542-3, 1567, 1640,
1653, 1656.

8) *Index of abbreviations used.* Some abstract journals which use abbreviations extensively in the text of the abstracts provide a special index of these.

9) *Index to classification.* This is usually omitted in favor of classification schedules in tabular form. But *Statistical Theory and Method Abstracts,* which provides a scheme for the classification of abstracts, also gives a separate "Analysis of secondary classification." The latter is arranged by the secondary classification number, followed by references to the main classification number used for the abstract concerned. *Sociological Abstracts* includes, in the annual volumes, a cumulative classified contents list showing the representation of each part of the classification in each issue by abstract numbers and by pages—thus some five thousand abstracts are classified under fifty-one subject sections.

10) *Index of institutions.*

Abington School District, Pa.
CAREER DEVELOPMENT ACTIVITIES.
GRADES 5, 6, 7.
                                    ED 022 219

Academy for Educational Development, Inc.,
New York, N.Y.
THE USE OF LIBRARIES AND THE CON-
DITIONS THAT PROMOTE THEIR USE. A
REPORT TO THE NATIONAL ADVISORY
COMMISSION ON LIBRARIES.
BR-7-0961
                                    ED 022 489

Air Training Command, Reese AFB, Tex.
3500th Pilot Training Wing.
EVALUATION REPORT ON THE AIRMAN
DEVELOPMENT COURSE.
                                    ED 022 133

Alaska State Dept. of Education, Juneau.
SCIENCE - CURRICULUM GUIDELINES
GRADES K-12.
                                    ED 022 711
STATEWIDE PLANNING FOR PROGRAMS
IN EDUCATION, ALASKA STATE DE-
PARTMENT OF EDUCATION.
                                    ED 022 587

11) *Analytical subject index to the abstracts.*

CUMULATIVE SUBJECT INDEX

A

Ability(ies)
conception of personality, 12:C3468
differential, on the Scholastic Apti-
tude Test, & social development,
32:C4483

scientist, sponsored & contest mobility of, 32:C6765
standards of sociology in Hong Kong,
02:C5456
standards of the two cultures,
32:C8530
status symbols, 06:C4695
streaming in a grammar school,
32:C3804

motivation theory, re vocational
choice & propensity for risk
taking, 20:C3732
motive re economic growth, 07:C4733
occupational & academic performance
in college, 32:C5988
of success goal, adaptations to
blocked means for, 07:C3411
orientation & its influence on the

of the family, & mental health, 46:C6186
of the Lapps of Finland, 14:C5673
plasticity & achievement in developing
economics, 15:C8218
response, human biological variation
as an, 44:C3865
significance of reduction in tooth size,
44:C5327
tactics in four Japanese groups, re

CUMULATIVE SUBJECT INDEX (CONTINUED)

resources, measurement of, 32:C6778
social class differences in, 32:C8532
Aborigines
Australian, demography of, 14:C5672
Mossi, emigration of, 14:C8147
Formosan, age organization & men's
house of the, 14:C8118
Formosan, field work among,
14:C8115
of Taiwan, cultural contact & the
change of economic life among,
14:C8145
Ojibwa, regional examination of
cultural history of, 14:C8146
Puyuma, of Taiwan, 14:C8143
societies, Formosan, 08:C8089
Abortion

subaltern, the assistant, 32:C7612
subculture re the sociology
of religion, 35:C8568
women, 20:C5870
world of women trained in engineering, 34:C7725
Acceptance
social, & compatibility, 12:C3429
Accident(s)
childhood, as a measure of social
integration, 38:C4565
liability among children, exposure-
coping model of, 38:C8649
& regularity in history, 03:C7916
Accommodation
conjugal, & bi-ethnical marriage
in Canada, 41:C6932

social & personal system, 12:C5544
& role definition of the college
student, 32:C4451
scientific, autonomy, coordination &
stimulation re, 34:C3849
social influence on, in four psycho-
motor tasks, 09:C5579
student, organizational influences
on, 32:C7639
team, re generation changes in,
42:C5803
test scores, secondary school students' & occupations of parents,
32:C6771
values, n achievement & socializa-
tion, 20:C8385
Acquaintance

utopian communities, 26:C6503
to blocked means for achieving a success goal, 07:C3411
Addict(s)(ed)(ive)(ion)
narcotic, Chinese, in the U.S.,
47:C3947a
narcotic drug, patterns of, in the U.S.,
47:C7883
Adjustment
agricultural, impacts & effects
of, 16:C8432
& attitude of Negro mothers in
single-headed households, 41:C4607
capacity & fatigability, assessing,
work microcurve re, 21:C4136
economic farm, in the Southwest,
16:C7545

Sociological Abstracts

This is the most important indexing feature of any abstract journal, though the amount of attention given to it, and the methods of constructing such an index have innumerable variations. The editor's aim is naturally to include in the analytical subject index every aspect to which he believes users might wish to refer. Thus, in many cases the abstractor is asked when abstracting an article to include recommendations for possible index entries. In the editing stage these may be amplified, altered, eliminated, or increased, since it is the task of the editor of the index to achieve both consistency and comprehensive coverage.

The index terms used are often divided into two classes:

    a) descriptors
    b) identifiers

The descriptors are those terms used for subject characterization which are included in the recognized thesaurus in use for the journal, or, if no thesaurus is in operation, are in general use in that subject-field. Thus new descriptors would have to be noted by the abstractor for consideration for approval or for incorporation in the thesaurus. Identifiers include project names, proper names, acronyms, names of organizations, code names, trade names, catch-titles, key-word and title-word items, etc., which would not be considered of sufficient analytical nature to be treated as descriptors. But of course there are many cases of new words, originally used as identifiers, which have gradually become accepted in general terminology and have qualified as descriptors.

In nearly every case the abstract journal will be found to have an alphabetical list of subjects mentioned in the abstracts, and this index may become very elaborate (as in the example above), though *Abstracts of Folklore Studies* provides only a brief index of subjects represented. In most cases the subject index headings are straightforward and similar in form to those in the now conventional indexes, but even here there can be variations. *Religious and Theological Abstracts* emphasizes its important subjects—The Bible, The Church, Church History, Denominations, Education, and Theology—by printing these headings in capitals. *Sociological Abstracts* has a particularly ingenious system of headings which may be related to computer exploitation: headings that are clearly related to variants are compressed into one heading, *e.g.:*

> Hebrew(aic)
> Republican(s)(ism)
> Phenomena(non)(al)(alistic)(ology)

and an even more elaborate form, where some variants are less important than others:

> Perception(s)(tual)(tivity)(ceive)(ceived)

The indexing method used is however highly individual, since in other parts of the index can be found differentiated items that might seem equally to be candidates for a similar process of compression, *e.g.:*

> Deviance
> Deviant(s)
> Deviant Behavior
> Deviation

It is this same journal that treats ethnic and similar subjects in a very individual way: "To facilitate location of tribes, societies, and similar large groupings (except religious groups), these have been indexed under the key term of: Society, the, of—in alphabetical order. Thus, Bantu will not be found under 'B' or Navaho under 'N', rather they will be found under 'S', *i.e.,* under the entry 'Societies, the, of.' "

12) *Continuity indexes.* The problem of connecting one abstract with another is one that has long preoccupied abstractors and the editors of abstract journals. An ingenious solution to the problem is exemplified by the example from *Documentation Abstracts* shown in the sample page. It will be noted that—as the key indicates—room is made for the exercise of a certain amount of judgment on the part of the abstractor.

CONTINUITY INDEX TO VOLUME 2

This index is intended to be a convenient guide to some of the important relationships between abstracts which have appeared in *Documentation Abstracts*. It is called a "continuity" index because such relationships may continue to arise or become apparent long after the initial publication of an abstract. The index design is experimental.

Comments from users are earnestly invited. This index supplements, but does not replace, the continuity index for Volume 1, which appeared on page 45 of the 1966 December issue. The Volume 1 continuity index contains relationships identified during 1966. The index below contains relationships identified during 1967.

KEY

Code letters indicate relationships between lightface abstract and the boldface abstract under which it is listed.

A — an application of (the boldface reference)
C — corroborates or affirms

VOL. 1 1966						
002	567	1060	67−002(Y)	138	67−176(N)	67−967(A)
67−1257(X)	67−835(V)	67−342(F)	Auth. Index	147	67−688(F)	264
003	67−886(N)	1106	67−342(E)	162	67−637(M)	67−331(MS)
67−406(N)	600	67−331(N)	67−688(E)	176	67−138(M)	269
014	67−342(F)	1123		189	67−491(X)	67−257(N)
67−358(A)	665	1151	VOL. 2 1967	190	67−656(X)	271
015	67−910(W)	1156	002			67−272(M)
67−358(A)	692	66−604(R)	66−1151(X)			272
67−706(N)	67−224(R)	66−795(R)	66−1192(X)			67−271(N)
	750	1177	66−1193(X)			279
	67−342(F)					67−280(S)
	783					67−281(S)

CONTINUITY INDEX (CONTINUED)

D – rebuts or rejects	116	66–343(M)	67–688(G)	66–1195(X)	67–563(R)	67–282(S)
E – erratum, corrects the original text of	67–761(A)	801	67–1327(G)	66–1196(X)	204	280
F – erratum, corrects the abstract of	158	66–802(S)	1180	66–1197(X)	67–192(R)	67–279(S)
G – provides availability data on	67–1327(F)	67–253(S)	67–1302(MV)	66–1199(X)	220	67–281(S)
M – a work continued by	172	802	1192	66–1201(X)	67–441(R)	67–282(S)
N – a continuation of	67–692(N)	66–801(S)	67–002(Y)	66–1202(X)	224	281
R – reviews, discusses, or compares	182	67–253(S)	1193	011	67–223(R)	67–279(S)
S – part of the same series or collection as	67–396(N)	952	67–002(Y)	67–047(R)	242	*67–280(S)
U – abstract is replaced by	194	66–532(U)	1195	025	67–1243(R)	67–282(S)
V – a different published version of	67–537(N)	953	67–002(Y)	67–026(S)	251	282
W – a replacement or supplemental abstract of	342	67–873(R)	1196	67–031(S)	67–1245(R)	67–279(S)
X – a portion of	66–343(N)	964	67–002(Y)	026	253	67–280(S)
Y – a composite work containing	343	67–342(F)	1197	67–025(S)	67–261(A)	67–281(S)
	66–342(M)	1006	67–002(Y)	67–031(S)	66–801(S)	331
	66–783(N)	67–482(N)	1199	031	66–802(S)	67–264(NS)
	411	1055	67–022(Y)	67–025(S)	257	66–1106(M)
	67–928(W)	66–269(R)	1201	67–026(S)	67–269(M)	338
	532	66–299(R)	67–002(Y)	034	261	67–1324(R)
	66–952(W)	66–1062(R)	1202	67–369(Y)	67–688(F)	342

13) *Keyword title indexes.*

ABELIAN
ABELIAN APPROXIMATE AUTO-
MORPHISMS (MATHEMATICS) 2544-B
ON THE STRUCTURE OF ABELIAN
GROUPS (MATHEMATICS) 2524-B
SOME RESULTS ON THE UNIQUENESS
OF TRIGONOMETRIC SERIES IN A
CLASS OF COMPACT ABELIAN
GROUPS (MATHEMATICS) 2535-B
ABILITIES
AN INVESTIGATION OF THE MODI-
FIABILITY OF VISUAL INTEGRATIVE
ABILITIES IN CHILDREN
(PSYCHOLOGY, CLINICAL) 2640-B
ABILITY
THE EFFECTS OF REHABILITATION
COUNSELOR TRAINING ON
ATTITUDES TOWARD THE DISABLED
AND ON THE ABILITY TO COM-
MUNICATE AND DISCRIMINATE THE
LEVELS OF FACILITATIVE
CONDITIONS (PSYCHOLOGY,
GENERAL) 2615-B
ABSENCE
EMBRYOLOGICAL EVIDENCE FOR THE
ABSENCE OF THE HUMAN
PREMAXILLARY BONE (ANATOMY)
2266-B

ACHIEVEMENT
DEVELOPMENTAL CHANGES IN
PERCEPTION AND REPRODUCTION
OF GEOMETRIC DESIGNS AND THEIR
RELATIONSHIP TO PRIMARY READING
ACHIEVEMENT (PSYCHOLOGY,
GENERAL) 2624-B
LEADERSHIP AND ACHIEVEMENT:
THE EFFECTS OF TEACHING STYLES
ON FIRST GRADE CHILDREN
(PSYCHOLOGY, EXPERIMENTAL)
2648-B
ACHONDROPLASTIC
CYTOGENETIC INVESTIGATION ON
NORMAL, INTERSEXUAL, LEUKEMIC
AND ACHONDROPLASTIC ANIMALS
OF BOS TAURUS (BIOLOGY-GENETICS)
2308-B
ACID
THE ACETOLYSIS OF P-METHYLBENZ-
HYDRYL ACETATE IN ACETIC ACID
(CHEMISTRY, ORGANIC) 2349-B
THE ACID CLEAVAGE OF ISOBUTENYL-
MERCURIC BROMIDE (CHEMISTRY,
ORGANIC) 2354-B
ACID-BASE EQUILIBRIA IN CONCEN-
TRATED SALT SOLUTIONS
(CHEMISTRY, ANALYTICAL) 2323-B

It will therefore be seen that, in order to use any abstract journal to the full, it is necessary to master the idiosyncrasies of its index or indexes. If this is not done, it is possible for the user to overlook the exploitation of valuable information. While the advisability of standardizing the indexing of abstracts can hardly be in question—and may sometimes be achieved —any such move would leave the volumes already issued still to be used by the methods of the older systems, for it is doubtful whether any re-indexing of their contents is likely to be done for a considerable period.

It must be admitted that the average user of abstracts has to deal with only one or two abstracting services for the most part, and he therefore quickly becomes acquainted with their indexing systems, however complicated or unusual they may be. The real sufferer is the researcher, usually a librarian or information scientist, who uses a large range of abstract journals in the course of his work. This may not always be the case since it has been noticeable that in the last few years scholars and research workers who are used to finding material in their appropriate abstract journals have ventured further afield in their quest for relevant items within the scope of their subject. In this way they have themselves become increasingly aware of the differences in method of the various abstracting services, and have also learned by experience that it is possible—even for one experienced in research methods—to fail to find material that has been included. So far, little investigation has been made of this problem; it is certainly one that is ripe for study, and schools of library science might well consider its possibilities for the new research programs they are now setting up.

PREPARATION FOR THE PRESS

An abstract should be a non-critical, informative digest of the significant content and conclusions of the paper, not a mere description.

BIOLOGICAL ABSTRACTS: Guide to the preparation of abstracts

It is the rare abstract journal that can allow sufficient time for a proof to be sent to the abstractor. Thus the editor and his staff are responsible for the text that is sent to the printer, and it is on them that the burden of seeing it through the press must remain. It is therefore in the interests of both the editorial staff and of the business manager that clean and well-nigh perfect copy should reach the printer so that the journal is published promptly, and in order that costs should be kept to a minimum. Any corrections—even if not charged to the journal—will result in delays and can sometimes cause further misprints. A glance at any page of an abstract journal will show how heavy is the responsibility of the editor and his staff, for within that page may be anything from five hundred to three thousand words, comprising three to twenty thousand characters, and even a margin of 0.1% errors could hold up the publishing process considerably.

To draw a line between the editorial process and preparation for the press is not always easy since, in the course of his editorial work, an editor may economically include some instructions to the printer. But, broadly speaking, editorial work comprises the standardization and classification of the abstractor's text and the addition of the necessary cross-references, index entries, prefatory matter, and so on; while preparation for the press looks ahead to the printer's problems and attempts to envisage and cope with those points on which he is likely to find any difficulty.

Thus uniformity of presentation is uppermost in the editor's mind. Each title, each reference, each cross-reference, each heading, and each sub-heading, must consistently appear in the same position and typeface throughout the current issue, and also in all former issues that have observed the same practice. In the case of many abstract journals the printer has standing instructions sufficiently detailed for him to follow this system without each part of each abstract being marked up in full. But in such a system there lies the danger of the mechanical approach, since the printer is following a practice which can deal correctly with variants only *if* the editor makes a definite attempt to call his attention to the exceptions that prove the rule. For example, in a name such as "ap Roberts" the printer, if he is unfamiliar with the custom of setting Welsh names, may automatically capitalize the "a" in "ap." Greek letters that can be mistaken for roman letters—*e.g.,* P, H, etc.—may be wrongly treated if the editor does not indicate in the margin of the text that the Greek letter is intended. A wordlike scientific symbol such as "He" at the beginning of a sentence needs either expansion or special setting.

The face and size of type used for abstracts is of the greatest importance, particularly since reproduction of the text is frequently necessary. A small type-face is not necessarily more difficult to read than a larger one, providing proper planning is available.*   But comparison of various current abstract journals will demonstrate the most astonishing variations in layout and typographical presentation. It is an axiom of the writing of abstracts that the abstract should be readable, but not every editor and printer of an abstract journal seems to have grasped that the abstract should also be clearly legible. In the interests of all concerned, the layout and typography of any new abstract journal should be planned well in advance by an expert, and specimen copies of a preliminary issue should be widely circulated for public reaction. These points apply even more to journals that are prepared in cold type or by photoreduction of typescript copy.

The more mundane matters of detail are also of the greatest importance. The cover of the abstract journal includes the masthead, the volume and issue numbers, the inclusive numbers of the abstracts included in that issue, and the month and year of publication. Most of these details must be changed in each issue—a task usually and confidently left to the printer, though it is still the editor's responsibility to ensure that this is done correctly. In addition, there may be details of contents, and, more certainly, of place of publication, and name of publisher—all of which may be subject to variation from time to time. On the spine there are similar details which are subject to minor variations. Within the cover, details are usually provided of the nature and policy of the issuing body and/or sponsoring organization, of the editor or editors, and of addresses of the organization's headquarters and branch offices, of the editorial offices, of the sales and advertising offices, and so on. Unfortunately information concerning frequency of issue, details of available cumulations and cumulative indexes, subscription rates, costs of individual issues, circumstances under which texts may be quoted or reproduced, and similar details are quite often omitted.

---

*   *The Times* (London) proved the point years ago with the planning and advice of Stanley Morison.

Even if the contents list is printed on the cover, it may appear again inside the issue. Though the general plan of this list may well be set up in advance, it is rarely possible to complete the list until the page proofs have been received and passed for the press, so that the finishing touches often have to be added at the last moment—thus increasing the danger of error. The continental practice of printing a standard comprehensive contents-page in each issue and of indicating by a box any parts of the classification not covered in the individual issue is being increasingly followed in the English-speaking world.

Following the table of contents there is often a list of periodicals abstracted, together with the abbreviations of their titles used in the text; in such cases, the list of periodicals is in two columns, of which the first comprises the abbreviation symbols. This list may either include new or recent additions (marked with a special symbol), or it may be followed by a separate list of titles newly added. It is equally important to indicate any journals whose contents are no longer being abstracted. Often the titles of the periodicals are given, with the volume and issue numbers and dates of those issues abstracted in the current number of the abstract journal; a very useful item of information that can save the research worker much time.

Some journals also include a list of abstractors, with details of their official position, and with or without their business addresses; this is sometimes placed at the end of the journal.

Often an outline of the classification scheme in use is provided, together with a brief guide to the principles on which it is constructed. This is sometimes combined with instructions for the use of the abstracts—a feature which is essential for any journal but not always present in every abstract journal. There may also be guides to the uses of the various indexes, though again, they may more helpfully be printed at the end of the abstracts so that users of the indexes become aware of their existence. The indexes are of course a vital part of the abstract journal and occupy a substantial proportion of its pages (sometimes equalling that occupied by the text of the abstracts). The detail in the indexes and therefore the likelihood of error is great. This necessitates special care on the part of the editorial staff, though the compilation of cumulative indexes provides a second chance to eliminate mistakes.

In spite of the care with which editorial work is almost invariably done, it is only when the page-proofs are received that some sources of ambiguity are noticed. Thus, a title displayed in print and in proximity to its neighbors may be seen to need amplification. Its setting may reveal that the text of an abstract requires some modification. Every editor knows that one entry, by its placing, can influence the reading or impression conveyed by other entries on the same or the opposite page, and this hazard of publishing is one that can never be completely eliminated. It is, in any case, essential to visualize the effect of the double-page spread.

In addition, in seeing the journal through the press, it is imperative to ensure that headings are satisfactorily continued from one page to the next, that continuous pagination and serial numbering of entries are correctly carried forward from one issue to the next, that awkward breaks in the text are avoided between one column or page and the next, and that everything is done to achieve the presentation of a coherent and helpful service.

A rather different aspect of publishing abstracts arises in cases where the abstract is printed on one of the preliminary pages of the original document, such as a report or dissertation. Here the abstract should include the full bibliographical citation, thus rendering the record completely ready for reproduction and incorporation in an abstract journal, and also identifying the abstract should it become detached from the document it accompanies.

Some journals, which feature abstracts of relevant items within their subject field, print them on pages whose versos are blank or bear only advertisements, so that they can be removed, mounted on slips or cards, and filed individually for reference. In this case, the type line should not exceed 10cm., and the type area should not exceed 103mm²., so that the abstracts will fit the standard filing card or slip of 7.5 x 12.5cm.

CUMULATION

The production of an abstract journal seems to be a continuing fight against error.

CHARLES L. BERNIER

Though the cumulation of abstracts in printed form is possible, the general policy of abstract journals is to cumulate only the indexes to each volume and, in some cases, to cumulate the annual indexes into multi-annual indexes. Thus, consultation of abstracts on a given subject may require reference to four or more separate parts of each volume. Most subscribers to abstracting services are so accustomed to this method of use, that the possibility of an improvement on the present system seems scarcely to have concerned them. But the introduction of automation has produced a new situation in which the physical cumulation of abstracts has become possible and, though their printed presentation in this form may not, in most cases, be thought economically feasible, their cumulation on disc or tape means that the relevant abstracts on a given topic will be available for considerable periods of the journal. This in fact constitutes an improvement on any existing service, and it already indicates the future method of use of abstracting services.

Whether or not abstracts are cumulated for printed presentation, or for recording on tapes or discs, the process provides an opportunity to achieve much more in the way of editing them than was possible in the rush of producing the individual issues of the abstract journal. For example, publication of an abstract may be followed by correspondence pointing out purely literal omissions or errors—such as wrong page numbers, etc.—or by objections serious enough to give rise to a reexamination of the abstract and some rewriting. Again, publication of the original article may have been followed by correspondence or further articles to which it is essential that attention be drawn. In addition, it may be possible to identify the authorship of articles originally published anonymously, or to establish additional details of use to subscribers to the journal. When the vast range of material handled by the average abstract journal is considered, it is surprising that cases of this type are not more frequent, and the high standard of maintenance of editorial control is clearly recognizable.

Furthermore, cumulation provides an opportunity for more detailed editing, such as the reclassification of abstracts, the elimination of inconsistencies and ambiguities, and the improvement of entries by linking them with related abstracts of importance:

> *cf.* 69/134; 69/139; 69/218 or
> *cf.* Johnson 69/134; Masters 69/139; Andersen 69/218

or the linking of whole series of abstracts (such as reports of a serial nature), where the original articles have been appearing regularly or irregularly in a numbered sequence over a period of time. The final decision on how to treat such cases may not become apparent until the whole series has been published: an entry for the "umbrella title" may then appear at one point, while the abstracts of the individual articles may be scattered according to subject coverage over a wide range of subjects in the cumulation of the abstract journal.

In the process of cumulation, inconsistencies unnoticed at the time begin to show and can be adjusted. Thus the wrong classification of abstracts may become apparent when seen in juxtaposition with other abstracts (an important point, since many users regularly turn only to those subject sections that particularly interest them), but what is far more likely to be noticed is the inconsistency in the awarding of index headings where these are included in the abstract entry. While it is true that many of the defects of abstracts are usually invisible to their users, the editorial staff is naturally sensitive to such matters and, in reviewing the cumulated material, editors develop a standard of judgment that, taken to a logical conclusion, could result in the revision of almost every abstract and its index entries!

The objects of cumulation must constantly be watched by the editorial staff, bearing in mind the type of future use their abstract journal is likely to have. This involves not only maintaining an internal consistency in the use of classification subject headings, and indexing, but also keeping in line with general trends. Since current research increasingly involves the consultation of several abstracting services, it is clear that uniformity in terminology is essential if important references are not to be missed. More importantly, there is the distinct possibility that attempts will be made in the future, perhaps on an international scale, to form data banks combining the contributions of many different abstracting services in the same and related subject fields. If such moves are made, the institution of uniform treatment and terminology will be an essential basis for their success. This applies to the bibliographical layout of entries, the treatment of forms of proper names, the abbreviation of periodical titles, the employment of symbols, and those details, discussed in previous chapters, in which variations occur. Unless these variations can be eliminated, the future of international cooperation seems dim indeed. International standardization is therefore urgent in the field of abstracting, but agreement may be slow in coming, for the chief abstracting services of each great nation are now well established and would face serious problems in adjusting their methods to the requirements of a universal standard. On the other hand, an international fund of abstracts makes a pool of common knowledge that could materially accelerate the advance of scholarship and discovery.

Cumulation also allows for the inclusion of relevant material from other abstracting services in the interests of completeness. The incorporation of abstracts from other journals by editorial agreement is a standard practice in a number of cases, and is a sensible way of increasing coverage and of eliminating wasteful duplication of effort.

Cumulation also provides an opportunity to include, in their correct position, abstracts that have been delayed for such reasons as the late receipt of journals (particularly those from overseas) or the illness or absence of abstractors. The publication of cumulations or of the cumulative indexes also provides an opportunity to give details of journals dropped and of new journals added since the publication of the last cumulation, and to add explanations of alterations to the classification, additions to the subject headings used, or other significant developments that have occurred during the preceding six or twelve months or so.

A cumulation is a formidable publication, and the addition of adequate explanatory material enabling the user to exploit its contents without error or oversight is most desirable. What may appear simple to the compiler may not be simple to the user. When it is recalled that, for example, *Biological Abstracts* alone now provides annually indexed references to about 135,000 internationally published research papers, covering some seven thousand journals from over ninety countries (and that *BioResearch Index* adds another eighty-five thousand entries or more), it will be recognized that explanatory aids are essential for everyone using the larger abstracting and indexing services.

Mathematical Reviews in 1940, so the 1945–47 gap in the *Zentralblatt für Mathematik* ... was minimized. Other important wartime abstracting developments included the inception of *Facts on File* in 1940; the issue of *Cancer Research* by the International Cancer Research Foundation (later, the American Association for Cancer Research); the start of the American Society for Metals' *ASM Review of Metal Literature,* now titled *Metals Abstracts;* the launching of *World in Focus* by the Library of International Relations, Chicago, in 1945; and the start of the British Ministry of Aviation's *Index Aeronauticus: Journal of Aeronautical and Astronautical Abstracts.*

The creation of the international non-profit making organization, the Excerpta Medica Foundation, in 1946, is one of the great events in the history of large-scale abstracting. This Foundation was established to further the progress of medical knowledge by making information available to the medical and related professions on all significant basic research and clinical findings reported in any language throughout the world. To accomplish this task, the Foundation set up an international biomedical communication system, with headquarters in Amsterdam, to screen, evaluate, classify, translate, abstract and index relevant scientific literature as it appears. More than 3,000 serials (comprising some 20,000 issues annually) are scrutinized, the complete journals being microfilmed (since 1960) in co-operation with the Royal Netherlands Academy of Sciences. At present the Foundation issues 34 English-language abstract journals monthly which are arranged according to a detailed classification scheme so that together they cover the entire medical field including:

Anatomy
Anthropology
Embryology
Histology
Anesthesiology
Arthritis and rheumatism
Microbiology
Bacteriology, virology, mycology and parasitology
Biochemistry
Biophysics, bio-engineering and medical instrumentation
Cancer
Cardiovascular diseases and cardiovascular surgery
Chest diseases, thoracic surgery, and tuberculosis
Dermatology and venereology
Developmental biology and teratology
Endocrinology
Gerontology and geriatrics
Hematology

Human genetics
Immunology, serology and transplantation
Internal medicine
Neurology and neurosurgery
Nuclear medicine
Obstetrics and gynecology
Ophthalmology
Orthopedic surgery
Otorhinolaryngology
General pathology and pathological anatomy
Pediatrics
Pharmacology and toxicology
Physiology
Psychiatry
Public health, social medicine and hygiene
Radiology
Rehabilitation and physical medicine
Surgery
Urology and nephrology

THE EARLY HISTORY OF ABSTRACTS

Abstracts provide the capability to concentrate within a single publication knowledge that is recorded in a multitude of research papers and technical reports.

IRVING M. KLEMPNER

On the 5th day of January 1665, Denis de Sallo, sieur de La Coudraye (1626–69), a magistrate and a friend of Colbert's, issued the first number of the first published abstract journal. It was called the *Journal des sçavans,* and it was issued weekly. There was no editorial, no statement of policy, and the contents of the first issue were like those of no other periodical. Approximately half of each page was devoted to a single item, usually a new book, though in some cases it was a decree, or an informative letter, and details were given of its author, title and place of publication. The journal was well printed, and it created a favorable impression with its partly abstract and partly review commentaries. With such a journal, the well-informed man could feel that he had a chance to keep up-to-date with intellectual developments throughout the whole of the civilized world, for the items noticed were not restricted to French publications, and there was a distinct international flavor that appealed to its international readership. The journal's appeal was in fact so strong that many other publishers followed suit and paid it the highest compliment by issuing similar periodicals. The age of abstracting had begun.

Sallo did not of course invent the abstract. This had always existed from the time when records first came into existence. Court officials had summarized state documents for the king and his ministers, ambassadors had sent back terse but vivid accounts of the events they had witnessed for the benefit of the governments they served, lawyers had long been in the habit of preparing case histories that seemed to provide useful precedents, and monks had calendared local happenings and national occasions in the margins of their manuscript histories of their Orders. But, Sallo did invent the abstracting journal, though his own contribution was limited to the first thirteen issues. His commentaries speedily offended the susceptibilities of the authors whose works he discussed and, in addition, he came into conflict with the Inquisition whose decrees he had dared to précis. Sallo refused to compromise by accepting the surveillance of a censor, and so found himself deprived of the official permit to issue his journal, and thus lost his right to edit it. Instead, the permit was transferred to the abbé Gaulois, a man far less energetic but, to the authorities, far more acceptable than Sallo. The *Journal des sçavans* survived without a break for at least another 130 years, and its long history is well worth studying.

The origin of the abstracting journal has often been regarded as specifically German, but in fact the next effort—the *Nouvelles de la République des lettres* (Amsterdam, 1684–1718)—was issued in exile by the great French philosopher Pierre Bayle (1647–1706), who had been inspired by Sallo's example. Similarly, another exile, the Protestant historian and jurist Henri Basnage, sieur de Beauval (1656–1710), a friend of Bayle's, issued the *Histoire des ouvrages des savans* (Rotterdam, 1687–1706; 1708–09).

The first German abstract journal was the famous *Monatsextracte,* which was issued from Leipzig from 1703 onwards. Unlike the *Journal des sçavans,* the *Monatsextracte* comprised a selection of important items from political journals, and thus more closely resembled a news summary. This was followed by the half abstract / half review journal, the *Deutsche acta eruditorum; oder, Geschichte der Gelehrten, den gegen-wärtigen Zustand der Literatur in Europa begreiffen* (Leipzig, 1712–39), a monthly journal issued by Johann Friedrich Gleditsch, which was superseded by the *Zuverlässige Nachrichten von dem gegenwärtigen Zustande, Veränderung und dem Wachsthum der Wissenschaften* (1740–57). And so, what has been widely quoted as the first authentic abstract journal, the *Aufrichtige und unpartheyische Gedancken über die Journale, Extracte und Monaths-Schriften, worinnen dieselben extrahiret, wann es nützlich suppliret oder wo es nothig emediret werden; nebst einer Vorrede von der Annehmlichkeit, Nützen und Fehlern gedachter Schriften* (1714–17), was really a comparatively late starter. This journal was edited by Christian Gottfried Hoffmann (1692–1735); it abstracted the contents of some forty periodicals.

At Erlangen the *Vollständige Einleitung in die Monaths-Schriften der Deutschen* first made its appearance in 1747. This journal comprised the contents-lists of periodicals issued in the previous year, and included extracts from some of the articles. In the same year the popular and long-lived English journal, the *Universal Magazine of Knowledge and Pleasure* (1747–1815) started publication, and was followed in 1749 by the *Monthly Review* (1749–1844) whose sub-title read: "a periodical work, giving an account, with proper abstracts of, and extracts from, the new books, pamphlets, &c., as they come out." Frankly modelled on the example of the successful *Universal Magazine,* the *Allgemeines Magazin der Natur, Kunst und Wissenschaften* (Leipzig, 1753–67) was entirely devoted to the contents of foreign publications.

In opposition to Elie-Cathérine Fréron's *Année littéraire* (1754–90), Pierre Rousseau (1716–85), in collaboration with the witty Nicolas Chamfort (1741–94), issued the *Journal encyclopédique ou universel* (Liège, 1756–59; Bouillon, 1760–93), a fortnightly that summarized European contemporary cultural developments. Representing the revolutionary ideas in the politics and literature of those days, it earned Voltaire's enthusiastic approval as the outstanding newspaper of its time. Mention must also be made of the short-lived *Journal des journaux; ou, Précis des principaux ouvrages périodiques de l'Europe* (January–April 1760), which was issued from Mannheim by a "société des gens de lettres."

The *Ausführliche und kritische Nachrichten von den besten und merkwürdigsten Schriften unsrer Zeit* (Lindau, 1763–65) was continued as the *Vollständige und kritische Nachrichten von den besten und merkwürdigsten Schriften unsrer Zeit, nebst andern zur Gelehrsamkeit gehörigen Sachen* (1765–69). The celebrated geographer Johann Georg Hager (1710–77), rector at Chemnitz, edited the bi-monthly *Geographischer Büchersaal, zum Nutzen und Vergnügen eröffnet* (Chemnitz, 1766–78) which may be termed the first specialized abstract journal, constituting as it did a periodical bibliographic handbook, abstract and review journal for the use of geographers. There was no other attempt to provide subject-specialist abstract journals for another fifteen years.

The *Neue Auszüge aus den besten ausländischen Wochen-und Monatsschriften* (1765–69), a weekly journal issued from Frankfurt-am-Main, was devoted exclusively to foreign publications in the fields of medicine, agriculture, politics, fine arts and literature. But the best known and most extensive periodical in this category was the *Esprit des journaux français et étrangers* (1772–1815; 1817–18), which was first published by the Société des gens de lettres de France at Liège in 1772, and subsequently issued in Paris and Brussels. At the turn of the century it was taken over by the same press at Bouillon that was responsible for the *Journal encyclopédique*. During the years 1803–04 only, it adopted the title of the *Nouvelle esprit des journaux*. The importance of this journal can be judged from the fact that by 1793 it already comprised a collection of 244 volumes, to which a four-volume author and subject index was added.

With the first issue of Crell's *Chemisches Journal für die Freunde der Naturlehre* (Lemgo, 1778–81), the age of the subject-specialist abstract journal had definitely arrived. The *Chemisches Journal* was the first of a series of abstracting services in the field of chemistry edited by Lorenz Florenz Friedrich von Crell (1744–1816), a distinguished professor at Braunschweig and subsequently at Helmstadt, and Göttingen. The emphasis was clearly on science and technology, a characteristic that has survived to the present day. Crell, undaunted by the brief life of his first journal, continued his work with the *Chemische Annalen für die Freunde der Naturlehre, Arzneygelahrtheit, Haushaltungskunst und Manufacturen* (Helmstadt and Leipzig, 1784–1803), which he supplemented with his *Beyträge zu den Chemischen Annalen* (1785–99) and his *Neues chymisches Archiv* (1784–91).

The *Analytical Review* (London, 1788–98) was published by Joseph Johnson and edited by the scholar and wit, Thomas Christie. One of the most influential journals of the last part of the eighteenth century, it encouraged and developed the esthetic concept of the picturesque. Its sub-title indicates its importance in the present context: "History of literature domestic and foreign, scientific abstracts of important works in English, notices or reviews of foreign books, criticism of new pieces of music and works of art and the literary intelligence of Europe." The revolutionary period in France caused some difficulties in the field of abstracting: the *Annales de chimie* (Paris, 1789–1815) was not published during the years 1793–97; and the *Journal des sçavans* came to a halt in 1792, to be revived briefly in 1797 by the Académie des inscriptions et belles-lettres, after which it did not resume publication until 1816. Its title was then modernized and it became the *Journal des savants.*

The first new abstract journal to make its appearance in the nineteenth century was the *Taschenbuch für die gesammte Mineralogie, mit Hinsicht auf die neuesten Entdeckungen* which started publication in 1807, and subsequently changed its name to the *Neues Jahrbuch für Mineralogie, Geologie, und Paläontologie* (Stuttgart, 1830–1949). The naturalist, Baron de Férussac (1786–1836) and the Société pour la propagation des connaissances scientifiques et industrielles started their *Bulletin universel des sciences et de l'industrie* (Paris, 1824–31) in 1824, which superseded the trial run of the *Bulletin général et universel des annonces et des nouvelles scientifiques* (1823).

The long history of the famous *Chemisches Zentralblatt* (1830–1970) began with the issue, by the Berlin Academy, of the *Pharmaceutisches Central-Blatt* (Leipzig and Berlin, 1830–49), which was superseded by the *Chemisch-pharmaceutisches Central-Blatt* (1850–55), and subsequently by the *Chemisches Central-Blatt* (1856–1906), after which it assumed the title of the *Chemisches Zentralblatt: vollständiges Repertorium für alle Zweige der reinen und angewandten Chemie.* By establishing this service the Berlin Academy set a standard and an example on which most of the successful abstracting services of the past 140 years have been modelled. It is interesting to note that the first attempts at abstracts in the field of mathematics made their appearance in Terquem and Gérono's *Nouvelles annales de mathématiques; journal des candidats aux écoles polytechniques et normales* (Paris) where abstracts were included in the issues for the first two years only (1842 and 1843). A sustained service in this category did not start until 1868.

Abstracting services were badly needed in law and medicine and were begun in the early nineteenth century. The *Law Journal Reports* (London, 1822–49), *The Jurist: Weekly Periodical Containing Reports in All the Courts* ... (London, 1837–66), and the *Law Times Reports* (London, 1843–1947) served the field of law. In medicine, the *American Medical Intelligencer: a Concentrated Record of Medical Science and Literature* (Philadelphia, 1837–42) appeared only to be superseded by the *Medical News and Library* (1843–79) which, with various minor changes of title, eventually became the *International Record of Medicine.* In 1845 both disciplines gained powerful adjuncts: the famous series *Manning, Granger and Scott's Reports of Cases in the Court of Common Pleas,* and W.H.

Ranking's *Half-Yearly Abstract of the Medical Sciences: Being a Digest of British and Continental Medicine and of the Progress of Medicine and the Collateral Sciences,* which was issued in both London and Philadelphia (1845–73). In the same year the Deutsche Physikalische Gesellschaft founded *Die Fortschritte der Physik* which had a superb run (Berlin; Brunswick, 1845–1918) until it was temporarily interrupted by World War I; in 1920 it was revived under the title of the *Physikalische Berichte* by the Verband Deutscher Physikalischer Gesellschaften.

Few people will consider a newspaper index as an abstracting service, yet a glance at the index of the *New York Times,* dating from 1851, will show that this magnificent guide to the world's events has all the ingredients of an abstract journal; detail, impartiality, conciseness, and comprehensiveness. Similarly, historians of the abstract have ignored the claims of statistical abstracts, yet scrutiny of the series of the British *Annual Abstract of Statistics,* whose first volume (1853) covered the preceding fifteen years retrospectively, will demonstrate that they are the purest form of abstract.

In 1856, under the auspices of the Königlich Ministerium für Handel, Gewerbe und öffentliche Arbeiten, Dr. Ernst Schubarth issued the retrospective volume (1823–53) of the *Repertorium der technischen Literatur,* a useful adjunct to users of abstracts, being a subject-index to some four hundred journals in the field of engineering. During the next ten years several legal series were started: the *Common Bench Reports* (1856–65) continued the work of *Manning, Granger . . . ,* the Incorporated Council of Law Reporting authorized publication of *The Law Reports in All the Courts* in 1865, and *English Reports Annotated* began in the same year.

The appearance of the *Jahrbuch über die Fortschritte der Mathematik* (Berlin, 1868–1944) confirmed the leadership that German scientists had established in the careful documentation of their subject-fields: the high standard of their work has remained the model of documentalists in other countries, and the only significant characteristic that has not been copied elsewhere may be said to be that of the use of highly-developed abbreviation of much-used words and phrases. In spite of the comprehensive German abstracting services there was a demand for English-language abstracting services, and in 1871 the Chemical Society began including abstracts in their *Journal,* and the Society of Chemical Industry followed suit in 1882. In 1873 the distinguished botanist Leopold Just (1841–91) founded the *Botanischer Jahresbericht: systematisch geordnetes Repertorium der botanischen Literatur aller Länder* and its excellence was recognized after his death by the addition of his surname to the title. It was published in two parts commencing with volume 6. The first part covered anatomy, morphology, and physiology; the second, palaeobotany, phytogeography, pharmaceutical and technical botany, and phytopathology. The *Nippon kagaku soran* (Chemical abstracts of Japan) were first issued in Tokyo in 1877, and, in 1878, the U.S. Government Printing Office published the first volume of the annual *Statistical Abstract of the United States.*

One of the world's outstanding series of indicative abstracts, the *Engineering Index,* was first issued in New York and London by the Association of Engineering Societies in 1884. Three other important series were also launched in the eighties: *The Times Law Reports* (London, 1884–1952), the *Abstracts* of the Linnean Society of New York (1888–1932), and the *Abstracts of Proceedings* of the Association of Life Insurance Medical Directors (New York, 1889–1940).

The final decade of the nineteenth century saw the start of a number of important abstracting services. The Laboratoire de psychologie physiologique de la Sorbonne first issued *L'Année psychologique* in 1894. The Physical Society began publication of their *Abstracts of Physical Papers from Foreign Sources* (London, 1895–97) which was continued by *Physics Abstracts,* i.e., Section A of the Institution of Electrical Engineers' *Science Abstracts.* Massachusetts Institute of Technology issued their *Review of American Chemical Research* (1895–1906) which was superseded by the American Chemical Society's *Chemical Abstracts.* The Centre de documentation chimique started the *Annales de chimie analytique* (Paris, 1896–1941) which was continued by *Chimie analytique.* The renowned astronomer Walter Friedrich Wislicenus (1859–1905), of the University of Strasbourg, founded the *Astronomischer Jahresbericht* which, since 1942, has been compiled by the Astronomisches Recheninstitut at Heidelberg. And the comprehensive *L'Année sociologique* (Paris, 1896–1912; 1923–25; 1940–48 to date) began its checkered career. During the years 1934–42 its work was covered by the *Annales sociologiques.*

Thus, in less than 250 years the main outline of abstracting services as they are now known had been fully accomplished. The general abstract journals, covering all aspects of science, culture and political events, did not survive the disappearance of the polymaths of the eighteenth century, and gradually they gave way to specialized abstracting services conducted by subject specialists. While such services attempted to be comprehensive and international in scope, the recognition that few people are gifted linguistically had resulted in similar services becoming established in different languages. It slowly became clear that one-man abstracting services, though often of a very high standard, were vulnerable; sooner or later they would perish if there were no provision for their continuance. Consequently, the enthusiastic and public spirited Crells and Justs must inevitably give place either to commercial publishers, or, since there was little or no profit to be made from issuing abstracts, to professional or learned societies. It was also clear that the main financial support for abstracts was only forthcoming from industry, and therefore the subjects covered tended to be those in which industry and commerce were vitally interested. So far, governments had played no active part in this field—except for the contentious examples of statistical and patents abstracts—and there were no international organizations or wealthy libraries to offer practical support. The traditions and the techniques had long been formed. The next developments must include wider and more sustained support and more intensive specialization.

TWENTIETH CENTURY ABSTRACTING SERVICES

The automatic abstracts derivable by present techniques require human editing to achieve adequate communicability.

SYSTEM DEVELOPMENT CORPORATION

In 1903 the Institution of Electrical Engineers issued Section B of their *Science Abstracts* under the title of *Electrical Engineering Abstracts;* Section C, *Control Abstracts,* which the Institution publishes in collaboration with the International Federation of Automatic Control, did not follow until 1966. In the years immediately preceding World War I, there were three notable developments in the field of abstracts. The American Gas Institute (later, the American Gas Association) issued their *Bulletin of Abstracts* (Easton, Pa., 1907–30), one of the first industrial services. The Institute of Metals published "Metallurgical Abstracts" (London, 1909–30) first as a supplement to the half-yearly volumes of their *Journal* and later (in 1931) separately. And the International Institute of Technical Bibliography published *Engineering Abstracts* (1910–13) as the English edition of the *Technische Auskunft* (the title of the monthly editions of the *Fortschritte der Technik*) thus constituting the first abstract journal issued in translation. It was also the first abstract journal to be issued by an international organization, for the *Bulletin* of the International Association (later, Institute) of Refrigeration did not appear until later in the same year.

The war years saw little new activity in the abstracting world: the Eastman Kodak Company started their *Monthly Abstract Bulletin* (Rochester, N.Y., 1915–61) which, with *Ansco Abstracts,* was merged into *Abstracts of Photographic Science and Engineering Literature* for which the Society of Photographic Scientists and Engineers and the Department of Graphics at Columbia University are jointly responsible. The Incandescent Lamp Department of the Nela Research Laboratory began an *Abstracts-Bulletin* (1917–30). And the Centre de documentation chimique launched a series of abstract journals covering chemical engineering, pharmacy, and cosmetics.

65

Immediately after the war a host of new services appeared: among them were the *Synopsis of Important Events* (1918–31), the precursor of *Keesing's Contemporary Archives;* the *Bibliographie géologique du Congo belge et du Ruanda-Urundi,* the Institution of Civil Engineers' *Engineering Abstracts,* and the *Referativnyi meditsinskii zhurnal* (Moscow, 1920–23), the first Russian abstract journal.

In the twenties the first real signs of growing official recognition of the importance of abstracts appeared with the publication by the US Public Health Service of *Abstracts from Recent Medical and Public Health Papers* (1920–22) which became *Venereal Disease Information* (1922–45), and of *Public Health Engineering Abstracts;* and with *Geological Abstracts,* started by the US Bureau of Mines and now issued by the US Geological Survey. Another development was the increase in activity by international organizations: The Industrial Safety Section of the International Labour Office introduced a "Revue des périodiques" in its *Chronique de la sécurité industrielle* in 1925; the International Association of Ice-Cream Manufacturers issued *Abstracts of Literature on the Manufacture and Distribution of Ice-Cream* (Harrisburg, Pa., 1927–34/35); and the International Institute of Administrative Sciences started the *Revue internationale des sciences administratives/International review of administrative sciences,* a journal which devoted a section to relevant abstracts. The growing independence of the countries of the British Commonwealth was reflected in the issue of *Abstracts of Proceedings of the Indian Central Cotton Committee* (Bombay, 1921–32) and of "Australian science abstracts" which were issued as a supplement to the Australian National Research Council's *Australian Journal of Science.*

There was also a tendency to publish abstract journals in new subject fields and to issue more highly specialized services. Thus, the Motor Industry Research Association started their *Monthly Summary: Abstracts of Automobile Engineering Literature; Mineralogical Abstracts* were initiated by the British Mineralogical Association (these have been published jointly in the USA since 1961); the National Canners Association issued *Abstracts of Canning Technology* (Washington, D.C., 1923–30); and, the *Anthropologischer Anzeiger: Bericht über die biologisch-anthropologische Literatur* was launched in Stuttgart by Rudolf Martin in 1924. The publication of abstracts of dissertations got under way at Stanford (1924), Cambridge (1925), Oxford (1928), and Ohio State (1929). But probably the most important event in abstracting history during this decade was the concern about the developing "information lag" which led the American Association for the Advancement of Science, the Union of American Biological Societies, and the National Academy of Sciences in 1926 to found *Biological Abstracts,* a journal that amalgamated *Botanical Abstracts* and *Abstracts of Bacteriology (BA).* Initially *BA* occupied an area made available by the University of Pennsylvania in its Zoology Department, and it was mainly supported by the Rockefeller Foundation. But in a few years the organization had become self-supporting and it now operates from Philadelphia, its present coverage comprising at least 135,000 published research reports and papers. In the same year *British Abstracts* carried on the abstracting functions of the journals of the Chemical Society and the Society of Chemical Industry; while in the next the American Psychological Association's *Psychological Abstracts* was founded; it included the functions of the *Psychological Index* (1894–1936) from 1937 onwards.

Government activity in the field of abstracts during the thirties was slight. The US Fish and Wildlife Service started the *Wildlife Review: An Abstracting Service for Wildlife Management* in 1935, but the most important move was the initiation of the *US Government Research and Development Reports* in 1938. Among the new services provided by the international organizations were the *Abstracts of Literature on the Production, Processing and Distribution of Fresh Milk,* issued in 1931 by the Committee on Laboratory Methods of the International Association of Milk Dealers; the International Council of Religious Education's *Abstracts in Religious Education: Selected Studies of Weekday Church Schools,* issued in 1934; the *Boletín bibliográfico de antropologia americana* of the Instituto Panamericano de geografía e historia (Mexico City, 1937–48); and, the International Institute of Philosophy's *Bibliographie de la philosophie* (Paris, 1937–39; 1946–53). India continued to develop abstracting services: the Indian Statistical Institute included abstracts in Series A of *Sankhyā: the Indian Journal of Statistics* from 1933, and the first comprehensive abstracting service, *Indian Science Abstracts (ISA): Annotated Bibliography of Science in India,* was started by the National Institute of Sciences in 1939; unfortunately it ceased in 1959 owing to lack of personnel and resources. Other important services started during this period include the *Zentralblatt für Mathematik und ihre Grenzgebiete* (interrupted during the years 1945–47); the *Abstracts of Doctoral Dissertations in Religious Education,* issued by the Bureau of Research and Survey of the National Council of Churches of Christ in the USA; *Animal Breeding Abstracts* from the Imperial Bureau of Animal Breeding and Genetics; the *Documentation économique* (interrupted during 1939–46) of the Institut national de la statistique et des études économiques; *Philosophic Abstracts* (1939–54); and, *Dissertation Abstracts* (now *Dissertation Abstracts International*) which, since 1966, has been published in two sections: A. The Humanities and Social Sciences, and B. The Physical Sciences and Engineering.

It is to France's credit that, in the middle of a major war, the Centre national de la recherche scientifique began and maintained its international abstracting service, the *Bulletin analytique* which, in 1956 changed its name to the *Bulletin signalétique*. From 1940 to 1946 the *Bulletin* abstracted only material in the mathematical, physical and biological sciences, but beginning in 1947 a third section covering the humanities was added. The latter was the first modern comprehensive service in this field. Ensured of survival by government support through the French Ministry of Education, this service has become one of the greatest abstracting services of modern times to which every major library subscribes. The American Mathematical Society fortunately started its

In 1969 the Foundation introduced a parallel series entitled *Classified Titles,* corresponding to the services listed above. The contents of these are classified according to the Excerpta Medica classification scheme, and are provided with monthly author and subject indexes which cumulate yearly. The computer-produced indexes differentiate between levels of importance in the subject entries.

Another product of the Netherlands in the same year was the *Documentieblad,* a weekly bulletin on tropical products in Dutch. The Advisory and Documentation Bureau of the Department of Agricultural Research at the Royal Tropical Institute in Amsterdam, gradually broadened the scope of this journal, so that by 1953 it had become an international English-language review of material on tropical and sub-tropical agriculture. At that time its title was changed to *Tropical Abstracts,* and it now covers agricultural products, forestry, animal husbandry, fisheries, economic aspects, the soil, etc. Also in the same year the US Atomic Energy Commission issued *Nuclear Science Abstracts* (titled *Abstracts of Declassified Documents* for the years 1947 and 1948), covering scientific and technical reports of the Commission and its contractors, those of other US Government agencies, and those of other governments, universities, and industrial and research organizations. The journal also covers patents, books, and journal literature on a world-wide basis. Scanning, selecting, and abstracting the literature in Canada, Denmark, Finland, Japan, Norway, Sweden, and the United Kingdom, are carried out by Atomic Energy Commission of Canada, the Danish and Finnish Atomic Energy Commissions, the Atomic Energy Research Insitute of the Japan Atomic Energy Bureau, the Institutt for Atomenergi, the Aktiebolaget Atomenergi, and the United Kingdom Atomic Energy Authority. Abstracts of European patents are provided through the Netherlands Patent Office and the Institut international des brevets. Sets of USAEC reports are maintained in depository libraries throughout the world. Other important new services included *Refrigeration Abstracts* (1946–57), founded by the American Society of Refrigeration Engineers in collaboration with the Refrigeration Research Foundation; the Institution of Civil Engineers' *Railway Engineering Abstracts;* the *Instrument Abstracts* of the British Scientific Instrument Research Association (SIRA); the *Bibliographie critique* of the Institut national d'études démographiques; the *Bulletin analytique de documentation politique, économique, et sociale contemporaine;* UNESCO's *Fundamental Education Abstracts;* and the *Australian Social Science Abstracts* (1946–54) issued by the Committee on Research in the Social Sciences of the Australian National Research Council. In 1949, the British and American editions of the *Engineers' Digest* were amalgamated.

The rapid increase in the creation of new abstracting services during the past twenty years is too voluminous to give in detail. Notable in the fifties are such new journals as *British Ceramic Abstracts,* the *Zentralblatt für Geologie und Paläontologie,* and *Library Science Abstracts* (1950); the *International Political Science Abstracts/Documentation politique internationale de sciences politiques* (1951) of the International Political

Science Association and the International Studies Conference; *South Asia Social Science Abstracts,* and the outstanding *Sociological Abstracts* (1952); and, in 1953, what Dr. A.J. Walford has rightly called "the most comprehensive abstracting service in the world," the *Referativnyi zhurnal* of the Soviet Union's Academy of Sciences, which appears in 24 series. This service is noted for the wealth of material (particularly in Asian languages) it abstracts, including the complete reproduction of charts, tables, etc., where they add significantly to the information contained in the text of the abstract. Only the poor typography and paper and the sparse indexes detract from the high quality of this major service. For the remainder of the decade there are the *Abstracts of Papers* of the Grassland Division of the Department of Scientific and Industrial Research of New Zealand (1955); *Historical Abstracts, 1775–1945,* the *Excerpta Botanica* of the International Association for Plant Taxonomy, the *Excerpta Historica Nordica* of the International Committee of Historical Sciences, and the *Personnel Management Abstracts* (1955); *New Testament Abstracts,* and the American Dental Association's *Dental Abstracts* (1956); *Tobacco Abstracts,* and *Standardization Abstracts* (1957); *Abstracts of English Studies, Religious and Theological Abstracts,* and *Indonesian Abstracts* (1958). It is also notable that 1958 saw the foundation of the National Federation of Science Abstracting and Indexing Services (NFSAIS), the first organization devoted to the interests of modern abstracting. The last year of the decade saw the start of the Society for Industrial and Applied Mathematics' *SIAM Review;* the American Geological Institute's *GeoScience Abstracts,* and the *International Journal of Abstracts: Statistical Theory and Method* issued by the International Statistical Institute.

In the last decade even more abstracting services have been started than in any similar period in the past. Among these are the *Bibliographie ethnographique de l'Afrique Sud Saharenne, dsh Abstracts* (issued by the American Speech and Hearing Association; dsh = deafness, speech, hearing), and, *l'URSS et les pays de l'Est* (1960); *Operations Research/Management Science: An International Literature Digest Service, International Aerospace Abstracts,* and *Excerpta Criminologica* (1961); *Abstracts for the Advancement of Industrial Utilization of Wheat, Corrosion Abstracts,* and *Abstracts of Papers of Oral Physiological Studies* (1962); *Journalism Abstracts, Abstracts of Folklore Studies, Science Abstracts of China,* and *Selected RAND Abstracts* (1963); *America: History and Life, Abstracts of Hospital Management Studies,* the *Oceanic Index* (possibly the only illustrated and certainly the most attractive of all abstracting journals), and *Mental Health Retardation Abstracts* (1964); *Industrial Ergonomics Abstracts, Abstracts for Social Workers,* and *College Student Personnel Abstracts* (1965). *Indian Science Abstracts,* which ceased in 1959, renewed publication in 1965.

In 1966 the US Education Research Information Center (ERIC) instituted a monthly abstract journal of the ERIC system called *Research in*

Education. This includes information about reports collected by the nineteen clearinghouses that comprise the national ERIC network, as well as the reports received from research projects funded by the US Office of Education. Users of this service can request from the central distribution center at Cleveland a microfilm or microfiche or hard copy text of the complete report abstracted in the journal. In the same year the University Council for Educational Administration started its *Educational Administration Abstracts,* and the Institute of Labor and Industrial Relations at the University of Michigan commenced publication of *PHRA: Poverty and Human Resources Abstracts.* Another notable addition in this year was *Documentation Abstracts,* sponsored by the American Documentation Institute, the Division of Chemical Literature of the American Chemical Society, and the Special Libraries Association. The institution of *BioResearch Index,* a monthly publication of BioSciences Information Service, was done to provide access to information that could not be presented in *Biological Abstracts* in the traditional manner. And the Department of Geography at the London School of Economics started *Geographical Abstracts,* which comprises four separate sections: A. *Geomorphology* (superseding *Geomorphological Abstracts*); B. *Biogeography, Climatology, and Cartography;* C. *Economic Geography;* and D. *Social Geography.*

In 1967 an interesting example of international co-operation in abstracting was first issued: *LLBA: Language and Language Behavior Abstracts* is edited at the Center for Research on Language and Language Behavior at the University of Michigan (CRLLB, Ann Arbor), in collaboration with the Bureau pour l'enseignement de la langue et de la civilisation françaises à l'étranger (BELC, Paris), and abstracts more than 600 journals from some twenty countries. Entries constructed at BELC in Paris are teletype-transmitted to Ann Arbor, for incorporation with those constructed by the CRLLB. Other new services set up in 1967 included *State and Metropolitan Planning Abstracts* (in which each abstract is mimeographed on a separate leaf), *Fluidics Feedback,* and the *RILM Abstracts of Music Literature* (RILM is an acronym for the Répertoire international de la littérature musicale). Its publication is serving as a pilot project for the American Council of Learned Societies' proposed interdisciplinary National Bibliographical Center. A service that broke completely new ground was the Argentine Naval Centre's *Resúmenes analíticos de bibliografía militar/ Abstracts of Military Bibliography.*

Recent new services include *Abstracts of Mycology* (the first specialist offshoot of *Biological Abstracts*); the US Food and Drug Administration's *Health Aspects of Pesticides Abstract Bulletin;* the TVA National Fertilizer Development Center's *Fertilizer Abstracts;* the Council for British Archaeology's *British Archaeological Abstracts;* the U.S. Department of Housing and Urban Development's *Abstracts of "701" Planning Reports;* the *Institute of Petroleum Abstracts; Food Science and Technology Abstracts,* sponsored by the Commonwealth Agricultural Bureaux, the Institut für Dokumentationswesen and the Institute of Food Technologists; and the *Cooperative Educational Abstracting Service (CEAS)* issued by UNESCO.

At a meeting held under the auspices of the American Council of Learned Societies on 19–20 June 1967, of fourteen editors of journals in the fields of interest of the Modern Language Association and of other subject specialists and experts, it was arranged that, beginning in 1967–68, all authors would be asked to furnish abstracts of an average length of two hundred words with the articles they submitted to these journals, and the editors agreed to forward these abstracts to the MLA office. In 1968 both *PMLA* and *Victorian Poetry* began printing author-abstracts together with the articles they published. It is planned in the near future to record *PMLA* author-prepared abstracts onto the same computer tapes from which it is hoped to print the *PMLA Annual Bibliography* and the ERIC bibliographies in foreign-language and English pedagogy. And in 1968 the Japan Information Centre for Science and Technology began to computerize the production of the nine subject issues of *Kagaku gizyutu bunken sokuho* (Current Bibliography on Science and Technology), thus reducing production time from three to one-and-a-half months, and speeding up production of author and subject indexes. After three years' accumulation of magnetic tapes generated by this system, it is hoped to make available a searching service (including other processed tapes) for public use.

In 1969 the American Petroleum Institute issued *API Abstracts of Petroleum Substitute Literature and Patents* and *API Abstracts of Air and Water Conservation Literature,* the British Cast Iron Research Association issued *BCIRA Abstracts of Foundry Literature,* the *Philosopher's Index* started publication, and the Institut für Raumordnung issued *Referate zu Raumordnung. Current Abstracts* [of medical literature], first issued in 1970, is printed on perforated cards for filing by subject; and the long run of *Chemisches Zentralblatt* (1907–70) has been superseded by an information service and a *Fortschrittsbericht;* while *Helminthological Abstracts* has found it necessary to divide into two journals: Series A. *Animal Husbandry,* and Series B. *Plant Nematology.* Commencing in 1971 *Historical Abstracts* plans publication in two parts, and expanded coverage from 1945 through 1970; Part A, *Modern History Abstracts,* 1775–1914, and Part B, *Twentieth Century Abstracts,* 1914–1970.

Thus, at the present time it appears there is no slowing up in the introduction of new and ever more highly specialized abstracting services. Another encouraging aspect is that the number of services that find it necessary to discontinue is now very small. There is clearly a much better market for abstracts than there was a few years ago. Indeed, this opinion is reinforced because some of the chief services have recently increased their charges significantly without too much protest. It is also noticeable that some of the largest services are beginning to provide for their specialist audiences by issuing "spin-offs" covering a limited field of their speciality, and by providing personal SDI services for organizations and individuals who are willing to pay for them. However, it is disturbing to note that, apart from mergers of some parallel services, little seems to be done to eliminate the overlapping coverage that results in some journals being abstracted in two or three different services, while a much greater number of periodicals are not abstracted at all. Also, there has so far been no move to study the overall coverage of abstracting services, with the object of defining those areas not served by any abstracting service. Such a study could only be carried out by an international organization—such as UNESCO or the FID—with sufficient resources not only to determine those gaps, but also with sufficient power and influence to ensure that they are filled as soon as possible. One more development remains to come: the retrospective abstracting of material that was issued before the institution of modern abstracting techniques.

MECHANIZATION

The intent of an abstract is to present the skeletal structure of the original and report the crucial findings or new processes the author presents.

SOCIOLOGICAL ABSTRACTS: User's guide

Mechanization of abstracts has already been achieved, although the full potentialities of this field have not yet been realized. Mechanization had its origins in the exploitation of the by-products of new methods of machine-reproduction. When editors of abstracting journals realized that conventional methods of printing contributed to the delays in the publication of abstracts they turned to the new systems that were beginning to take the place of conventional hot-metal typesetting. These included various methods that substituted one hand process for several, so that the same process that typed the original entry also manufactured a tape that could convey to the machine instructions culminating in the production of the printed product. Thus, the actual process of producing the printed journal was accelerated and the time-gap between the writing of the original book or article and the publication of an abstract relating to that work was reduced.

But the tape, once produced, had further uses. At the time of typing the abstract, instructions could be fed into the machine concerning its indexing as well. And thus the index to the journal could be produced at the same time and, moreover, the tape could be utilized to cumulate the various issues of the journal at frequent intervals and to produce cumulative indexes as well.

These highly sophisticated techniques are commonplace in the more advanced abstracting organizations, although it will still be some time before all abstracting journals make use of them. Even so, the process of mechanization has developed far beyond this point, and this too is due to further exploitation of the original tape, a measure which also contributes to the economy and efficiency of the enterprise, since the more by-products that the original tape can be made to produce, the greater the lowering of cost of the individual processes.

The original input is frequently on a paper tape and from this the data can be transferred to magnetic tape. Thus, both the abstract and its index entries and cross-references appear in a form suitable for machine processing. A file of these tapes can be made of permanent value by intelligent searching of their contents. Thus an abstract or its title may not include some of the terms or phrases used for indexing purposes. On the other hand it will include several words and phrases *not* used in the index entries, as a glance at the abstracts in *e.g., Sociological Abstracts,* will show. Therefore a thorough search of both index entries and of the actual texts of the abstracts can reveal more information than users of the printed abstracts would be able to obtain in many hours of perusal. It might be said at this juncture that a similar search of the tapes of the original articles in journals entirely photoset—such as the *Journal of Chemical Documentation*—would reveal much more but this, at the moment, is such an expensive process that it must await the day when machines can "scan" printed texts instead of laboriously "reading" them as is necessary at the moment.

The present form of mechanization, by which a search can be programmed for the actual texts of the abstracts promises future development. Indexing must necessarily be based on current concepts of what future research is likely to need, but however intelligent such indexing may be, it is necessarily fallible and cannot possibly legislate for all the viewpoints of the future. Future needs can be partly met by searching the abstracts themselves for words and phrases whose full future significance the indexer could not appreciate, and in that way provision for what truly is being overlooked in the indexing process can be at least partially ensured for the future.

But the future of mechanization may well go further. Experiments plainly reveal the planners' thinking. The features of abstracts are being analyzed in terms of their application to mechanically handled data. Another approach requires an article to be abstracted independently by several persons, and then each sentence of the original article is coded and the comparative choices of individual sentences analyzed for inclusion in the abstracts. A third and less tangible system analyzes the recognizable and appropriate attributes of sentences, of paragraphs, and of entire articles, categorises and codes them, then tries to identify those suitable for inclusion in an abstract. The difficulties and dangers of such measures are obvious but, in an age where mechanical translation from foreign languages is not admitted to be impossible, it would be a foolhardy man who believed that out of such initial attempts, something more practical may not eventually emerge.

THE FUTURE OF ABSTRACTING SERVICES

Abstracts should never be used as primary sources.

BRITISH ARCHAEOLOGICAL ABSTRACTS

The future of abstracting and abstracting services should prove very interesting. In the past few years abstracts have established themselves as an essential part of everyday life: the failure of abstracting services owing to lack of interest and support—a familiar feature of the thirties and forties —is now a thing of the past, and while established services continue to expand and develop in size and complexity, the number of new services is also still increasing. It is not easy to estimate the total size of this aspect of the information industry, but it is probably a conservative figure to put the number of people actively engaged in producing abstracts—mostly on a part or spare time basis—at half a million.

While the continued existence of abstracts is not at stake, their continuance in the forms in which we now know them is doubtful. The changes, which appear inevitable, seem ultimately to promise considerable improvements in service, though the transitional stages may prove disconcerting. These changes, which have in some cases already started, are due to a combination of factors which, each minor in itself, are together capable of altering the whole structure of abstracting.

Questions of finance, though not the chief factors in abstracting developments, are bound to play a big part in the immediate future of abstracting services. While the quality of abstracting services has, in general, continued to improve, their financial backing has continued to deteriorate owing to the rapid rise in costs of manpower and production. While many abstracting services have relied on recognition of the quality of their product and on the natural growth in numbers of users (such as new libraries) to bring them the steady and substantial support that would eventually make them self-supporting, this has rarely happened. There are few private subscribers to abstracting services, and those who have bought their publications have been in the main libraries, educational and research establishments. These have naturally been resistant to steeply rising charges and have tended to limit their support (*e.g.,* by cutting the number of additional copies purchased to counteract increases in subscription rates) at a time when it was most needed. The financial structure of abstracting services has in fact in some cases proved unsound and their survival has often depended on generous subventions from the general funds of professional or learned societies and other organizations with interests in the subject fields concerned.

The difficulty seems to have arisen through failure to examine the purpose and functions of abstracting services. Initially, practically every abstracting service constituted an attempt to serve its readers by keeping them informed of new developments and happenings within their subject fields. This could be achieved by exerting a process of selection that could result in a publication which need not be large nor require a steadily increasing amount of space for its contents. The trouble began when this primary selective function was overlaid by the desire to provide a comprehensive service that intentionally omitted nothing. The motives that led to this change of policy are admirable and must be applauded since they envisaged the needs of the future as well as those of the day. On the other hand, by switching from a service that catered to a public whose needs could be fairly accurately estimated and met, to one which was inevitably impelled to perform or at least include an archival function, the costs were bound to grow without any proportionate benefit to the subscribers. Thus it is possible for there to be two very different estimates of the same service. It is reasonable for the editor to say that each abstract costs the subscriber only a fraction of a penny, while the user can say with equal reason that each abstract costs him a very much larger sum. Both are correct, since the editor is talking about the total number of abstracts, while the subscriber is referring only to those that have been of use to him personally.

Comprehensiveness, as an editorial policy, is here to stay since it obviously serves both national and international interests. The question remains concerning who should pay for such a policy which involves a steady rise in costs each year, since the world's output of periodicals is rapidly increasing. The answer appears to be that adequate support can only be derived from five sources:

1. International organizations
2. National governments
3. Industry and commerce
4. Relevant societies and organizations
5. Subscribers and users:
   a) individual
   b) libraries, educational bodies, etc.

Similar to the way in which universities set up new departments and the way research organizations set up new projects without making provision for an adequate increase in library finances and facilities, so government, commercial and industrial organizations often set up extensive research and development schemes without making financial provision for publication of the results. Even if such work is published, no allowance is made for the cost of its subsequent abstracting and indexing, nor for its publication or storage in this form.

Thus the burden of costs falls on individual subscribers, libraries and educational bodies—an unfair burden since, by this system, they are compelled to pay for abstracting everything rather than for what they essentially need. A fairer distribution of the costs would be to get government, business organizations and the societies to pay for the initial costs of abstracting and indexing and the continuing costs of storage, while the costs of retrieval of information for particular users should be passed on to the individual and library subscribers.

This redistribution of costs requires a change in thinking on the part of all concerned—sponsoring organization, research worker, publisher, abstracting service, and users—but it will be recognized that unless some such system is generally adopted, many abstracting services will continue to limp along financially—with consequent risk of losing good staff—at a time when they should be consolidating their position and planning further developments of service to their users.

Without finance, abstracts would not be published; without abstractors no abstract would ever be written. The present position is unsatisfactory, not because of a lack of suitable abstractors, but because of the inevitable delays that accompany any system dependent largely on voluntary labor. There are powerful arguments against the use of author abstracts, but these have been greatly reduced by the introduction of a system in which the author's abstract is successively reviewed by a subject-specialist referee and by the editor of the abstract journal, both of whom are concerned only that the abstract represent the original article accurately, succinctly and effectively. Since the abstract must be delivered at the same time as the text of the article is submitted, the average delay in obtaining the final text of the abstract is considerably reduced. The advantages of this method outweigh the disadvantages so greatly that some major abstract journals include more than 50% author-produced abstracts. An additional advantage, of which little use has so far been made, is the possibility of publishing abstracts in advance of the issue of original articles—a means of overcoming the sometimes very considerable delays that occur in getting work published in learned journals, owing to their growing backlogs of items already accepted for publication.

If there were no abstractors there would be no abstract journals. If there were no subscribers, there would be very few users of abstracts. Since there are few individual subscribers to abstract journals, access to abstracts must be mainly through libraries and quasi-library services. Here the rapidly growing subscription rates of abstract journals militate against their full exploitation. There is no library service in the world that does not have to reject some desirable material on the grounds of cost. The smaller the library—or the smaller the organization—the more desirable it is that access should be provided to comprehensive services listing and describing items that the library or organization cannot provide from its own resources, but which it can obtain on behalf of its users. Unfortunately, this is a policy to which only lip-service is usually paid. The largest libraries subscribe to abstracting services, the smaller libraries regretfully decline to do so. They prefer to purchase the more primary materials their readers also need, and rely on their wealthier neighbors to make good the deficiency.

In such circumstances there are several possible solutions. Some abstracting services have tried to meet the problem by offering special discounts to non-profit-making or educational organizations: an admirable policy but one that has reduced their financial powers at a time when they badly need a large margin for research and development. Another solution is the voluntary cooperation of neighboring libraries which, though it may achieve a far better coverage *in toto,* enforces an artificial system of distribution of abstract journals that compels users to visit several libraries at the same time that it prevents effective comparison. A better solution is the provision of government subsidies for this purpose in exchange for complete public freedom of access. This solution requires that the usual choice of sites must be the university and large public libraries whose generous hours of opening, substantial reading space available, and trained staffs, are most likely to meet the needs of would be users. After all, the costs of preparing and issuing abstracts are so high that anything less than 100% use is a sign of inefficient organization of information sources.

Even if the abstracting services are made fully accessible it is up to those benefited to use them. There is a natural resistance to any kind of new information service partly due to a healthy scepticism concerning new-fangled ideas, and partly due to a feeling of being satisfied with what has hitherto been available. It must be added that many people who could benefit from abstracting services are initially unaware of their existence and, when the abstracting service is finally discovered or otherwise drawn to their attention, they still have little idea of its full capabilities, or even of its coverage and arrangement. This is more noticeable in the case of technology than in the scientific areas. The fault lies largely in the lack of initial training in this field given to both scientists and technologists, and this will remain a formidable hurdle under the present educational system.

The right time to acquire knowledge of the resources and methods of using abstract services is while attending the university, but the effect of such training loses part of its force if the scientists and technologists among whom the new graduate first works make little use of these aids. The mere increase, or unfortunately, the initiation, of bibliographical instruction at universities and technical colleges will not remedy the situation completely, since many employers and employees remain unconvinced of the value of abstracting and indexing services. To achieve better understanding, more needs to be done to reach established scientists, technologists, and scholars: they can be reached through professional journals, conferences, meetings, etc. Even now, many readers of *The Times* (London) do not realize, when they glance at that very interesting feature "Science Report" that they are reading an effective, documented form of abstract. Similarly, in reading technical journals the subscriber finds many brief paragraphs and other miscellaneous material of great interest which, if not formal abstracts, approach that standard very nearly. Part of the resistance to abstract journals may stem from their uncompromising form and layout. A glance at any issue of *Oceanic Index* will demonstrate that abstracts can be attractively produced.

But for the practicing research worker to be fully convinced of the value of abstracts more studies in depth must be made to ascertain what the readers really want. Many users of abstract journals turn merely to the section that applies to their own particular area of interest; the rest of the journal, as far as they are concerned, is waste material whose value to others they may well appreciate without wishing to help pay for it. The days of the type of man who read completely through an abstract journal are past—if they ever existed in this century—and there is clearly a need for services tailored as far as possible to individual requirements. Moreover, the frontiers of the various subject areas are breaking down rapidly: the physicist may need to refer to *Biological Abstracts* as well as *Physics Abstracts,* the engineer may need a whole range of items from various abstract journals, and the sociologist may want abstracts in the fields of education, history, and psychology in addition to the invaluable *Sociological Abstracts.* And each, in so doing, is hoping for comprehensive coverage of these areas—an assurance he is hardly likely to get at the present time.

The fulfillment of such needs presents the editors of abstract journals with some formidable problems. If they can meet them, the financial difficulties they now face will certainly tend to disappear, for no one will refuse to pay for a service that results in saving many times its cost or which eliminates the repetition of research already done elsewhere. The question is: how this is to be achieved? The well established abstract journals have already arranged interchange systems ranging from mere blanket permission to copy each others' abstracts, to full scale exchange of tapes. But this goes only part of the way. Copying relevant abstracts results in bulking out journals, in redundancy, and in ignoring other material that awaits abstracting and detailed indexing. Services tailored to specific requirements, services that can be adjusted to meet the continually changing aims of the groups involved, are needed. To achieve this on a cooperative basis means that the editors of abstracting services must agree on standard forms for bibliographical references, abbreviations of titles of periodicals, arrangement of the text of abstracts, their format, etc. Though this is difficult to achieve on a national basis, it is comparatively simple compared with establishing the widely-desired cooperation on an international scale, which involves additional problems such as different systems of transliteration, dating, definitions of technical terms, etc.

It is becoming increasingly obvious that international cooperation is imperative. Knowledge knows nothing of geographical or political boundaries, nor can the West remain confident any longer that significant advances will not be made in other parts of the world. Complete and prompt exchange of information between all countries is the ideal, and could do much to eliminate the present time lag in the processing of most foreign language items. There are six principal languages of the world, and it is true that most outstanding material continues to appear in one or another of those languages—but this is a situation that can soon change, and provision restricted to materials in those languages merely helps users to overlook other items that can be of importance to them. International harmonization of glossaries, thesauri, and key-words, the standardization of indexing procedures and references, and the elimination of known areas of ambiguity—such as those described in "*Excerpta Medica* master list of medical indexing terms (Malimet)"* must be made in an effort of voluntary coordination before the real work of collaboration can be put on a firm footing.

If abstracting services to users are to prove fully effective, there must be better and faster means of access to the original documents. Those services that already offer rapid access report an increasingly greater response in spite of the present fairly heavy cost of copies. When documents are stored on microfilm, such a service is not difficult to provide, and it would appear that a common feature of abstracting services in a few years' time will be large data banks of original documents on which users can draw freely. Such services will make the task of the smaller libraries much easier, since such transactions can take place direct between customer and supplier, providing access to the abstracting journals is ensured by those libraries in the first place.

Even this kind of intensive service does not go far enough; the individual research worker may need only a table, an illustration or a diagram, without even being certain of its existence or, if he is, of its source. Much more analysis of the contents of periodical articles therefore needs to be provided and this can be achieved by computerizing abstract information providing the need for individual items is foreseen and planned in terms that the computer can understand. Here again, the computerization or microfilming of abstracts offers unlimited possibilities for retrospective searches, which is an expensive business whose costs will be more than retrieved in the case of success, and at least somewhat reduced in the case of negative searches. The computer is already being used for both hot metal and photocomposition of abstract journals and the tapes manufactured for this purpose are available to provide the additional services the user requires.

In abstracting services much depends on the quality of the indexing. At the moment there is more bad than good indexing and there is much

---

Excerpta Medica Automated Storage and Retrieval Program of Biomedical Information, 1969, pp. 9-13.

redundancy in this field. With all its faults, computer indexing appears to answer the needs of the future because it eliminates human variations in standards of performance and it produces indexes that can meet a production program. It also provides the means for constructing cumulative indexes that can greatly reduce searching time. But to do its job properly, computer indexing needs much more research to be done on the problems of the user and on his real needs. Anyone who has used an index constructed on the KWIC system will appreciate how much must be done before the task of searching such indexes becomes anything less than disagreeable.

Research institutions are scattered over a wide area and, as the frontiers of science and technology advance, they tend to find themselves in remote parts of the world in some cases. The day when the inhabitant of a large city could expect to find better research facilities there than those available to the man who dwells in a distant part of the country must surely vanish. With the growth of central data banks it should soon be possible to serve distant or scattered organizations through on line computer services equally well as though they were in the heart of the metropolis, particularly if land line television facilities can be added.

The recent appearance of a new class of "awareness" journals such as:

Current papers on control
Subject index to current literature on air and water conservation
Fast announcement service (US Clearinghouse for Federal Scientific and Technical Information)
Plastics industry notes
Selected current aerospace notices
B.A.S.I.C. (Biological abstracts)
Chemical titles (the first—1961—computer-produced index in this field)
Chemical-biological activities
Polymer science and technology
Current papers in physics
Current contents: physical sciences
Current papers in electrotechnology

shows that there is a growing demand for services anticipating the publication of abstracts. Users need to know at least of the published existence of a paper on such-and-such a subject by such-and-such a man—if such notices can be roughly classified and indexed, so much the better. As Mr. Foster E. Mohrhardt has pointed out,*

"Abstracts were originated to provide scholars with a convenient means of coping with increasing quantities of publications. Now abstracts themselves have become so voluminous that specialized indexes often replace the use of abstracts by those who need up-to-date and speedy access to publications."

---

*Library Trends, 16 (3), January 1968, p. 303.

Such services help to overcome the time lag before the appearance of the actual abstract and, if they are on tape, can be made sufficiently flexible to supply the varied needs of diverse groups. Secondary to abstracting services, they are fast becoming a vital bridge between the user and the immediate information he needs.

The automatic writing of abstracts is not yet in sight and there is a growing need for good abstractors and good indexers—for the computerized index only demands a higher degree of skill from the indexer who must now substitute foresight and planning for the mechanical drudgery he has had additionally to perform in the past. To ensure the supply of able indexers and abstractors, it will however be necessary to offer them a better status and a better standard of remuneration than they have achieved in the past. It is on record that a man stood by the printing-machines of one famous daily newspaper, his sole duty being merely to listen to the machines. Nevertheless, he was highly regarded, for his experience and judgment enabled him to detect any imminent fault from the slightest alteration in sound—the kind of fault which if unchecked, could put the machines out of action. Similarly, the abstractor and the indexer are vital links in the complex chain of communication—as long as they are generally regarded as clerical workers of no particular standing, the chances of recruiting the type of experts really needed are small.

An abstractor should be something of a documentalist and something of a subject-specialist. Thus, if a qualified engineer is recruited for this work, he needs to be given additional training as a documentalist; if a documentalist is recruited, he needs to be encouraged to increase his basic knowledge in relevant subject areas, so that he is fully familiar with the practices and jargon and technical language of those fields. The jobs that attract good men are those which offer possibilities of moving on to more important posts. This kind of incentive can be provided by the national and international organization of abstractors and indexers into a distinct profession that has its very senior opportunities as well as its large body of "middle" jobs on good salaries. At the moment there is no such nationally recognized professional body nor any scheme of training and qualification for abstractors and indexers. This situation needs to be remedied if a good supply of skilled technicians is to be forthcoming and maintained. Greater public recognition of the importance of the abstractor and the indexer will follow rather than precede the development of the great abstracting services of the future.

This is a fascinating subject and fortunately it has attracted the attention of some of the most original figures in the field of documentation. For those who wish to pursue this subject further, two recent publications can be confidently recommended to their attention. The January 1968 issue of *Library Trends* was, under the able editorship of Mr. Foster E. Mohrhardt, devoted entirely to the subject of "Science abstracting services— commercial, institutional and personal." And in 1969 the long awaited report of the Committee on Scientific and Technical Communications of the National Academy of Sciences and the National Academy of Engineering (SATCOM) was published under the title of *Scientific and Technical Communication: A Pressing National Problem and Recommendations for Its Solution.* It is pleasing to see that the Committee's report very largely endorses many of the points made by Mr. Mohrhardt's contributors. Though both of these works are devoted to the fields of science and technology, much of what they describe, criticize, and recommend applies equally well in other areas such as the humanities and the social sciences. Together they constitute a very readable and formidable argument for closer attention to one of the most important means of scholarly communication today.

APPENDIX

I. Abstracting Services

II. Selected Readings on Abstracts and Abstracting Services

ABSTRACTING SERVICES

Abstracts were, of course, strongly opposed by those who felt that if God had intended them to publish abstracts they would not have published full papers in the first place.

DEREK DE SOLLA PRICE

At least a thousand abstracting journals are now being issued, and every year those that fail for lack of support are more than replaced, numerically, by new ventures. Below are listed some five hundred past and present abstracting services: these will give some idea of the vast range of material now being covered, and a careful study of the various titles will reveal some of the trends in current policy in this field. It will be noticed that international collaboration between institutions with similar interests is increasingly the rule. It will also be observed that national summaries of scientific and technological effort are growing in numbers and that many of them are being issued in the English language. The comparative paucity of abstracting services in the humanities will be only too apparent, and the short lived efforts of the earlier years stand as monuments to warn off the venturesome. Other reflections will doubtless be made by the observant reader, but even the most casual glance will elicit that what has been covered is greatly outweighed by the subjects that have never been tackled.

The dates given relate solely to the inclusion of abstracting services and do not necessarily indicate the full life of an individual journal. Such information is readily available elsewhere, so that here it is possible to concentrate instead on the effective periods covered by the abstracting services. The list is in alphabetical order of title of journal; while, incidentally, the titles themselves reveal what is available on a subject, reference to the subject entries in the Index will guide the reader to other items that may interest him. Similarily, issuing bodies have been included in the Index for the convenience of the reader who knows of the existence of an official abstracting service without knowing its exact title.

Details of publication—publisher, place of publication, subscription rates, etc., have not been given for commercial services, as these are readily available for current materials in the national directories of periodicals. Where a service is issued by a government agency, international organization, professional or trade association, or other non-commercial entity, this fact is usually indicated together with the city in which the organization has its headquarters, since these services are often omitted from the trade directories. In the case of services that have been discontinued, further details will be found in the union lists of serials, the histories of periodicals (such as the great *Hatin* for French journals) and the general histories of scholarship that appear on the shelves of all good reference libraries. It will be noted that an attempt has been made to indicate the merging and succession of abstracting services, but the bewildering changes of title, sometimes over a very long period of time, have led to some omissions in this respect. To ascertain whether additional abstracting services in any particular subject are now available, it is suggested that an inquiry should be addressed to the appropriate professional or trade association.

AAVSO Abstracts (American Association of Variable Star Observers. Cambridge, Mass.), 1960–
AIA Abstracts, 1970–
APCA Abstracts (Air Pollution Control Association. Pittsburgh), 1955–
API Abstracts of Petroleum Substitutes Literature and Patents (American Petroleum Institute. New York), 1969–
API Abstracts of Refining Literature (American Petroleum Institute. New York), 1968–
API Abstracts of Transportation and Storage Literature and Patents (American Petroleum Institute. New York), 1968–
ASCE Publications Abstracts (American Society of Civil Engineers. New York), 1966–
ASM Review of Metal Literature (American Society for Metals. Cleveland), 1944–67 (continued by *Metals Abstracts*)
ASTIA Technical Abstract Bulletin (Armed Services Technical Information Agency. Arlington, Va.), 1957–
The Abstract and Brief Chronicle of the Time, 1782
Abstract Bulletin (Aluminium Laboratories, Ltd. Kingston, Ontario), 1929–59
Abstract Bulletin of the Institute of Paper Chemistry (Appleton, Wis.), 1930–
Abstract Journal: Scientific and Technical Information (Academy of Sciences of the USSR. Institute of Scientific Information. Moscow), 1966–   (English-language edition of the *Referativnyi zhurnal*)
Abstract of Literature on the Production, Processing and Distribution of Fresh Milk (Committee on Laboratory Methods, International Association of Milk Dealers), 1931–34 (continued by *Abstracts of Literature on Milk and Milk Products*)

Abstract of the Literature of Industrial Hygiene and Toxicology (supplement to the *Journal of Industrial Hygiene and Toxicology*), 1919–

Abstract Review (National Paint, Varnish and Lacquer Association. Washington, D.C.), 1928–

Abstracta Dermatologica (*Excerpta Medica,* Section 13), 1965–

Abstracting Service of Occupational Health and Safety Literature (International Labor Office. Washington, D.C.), 1950–

Abstracts for Recent World Literature on Chronic Bronchitis and Allied Conditions (Beecham Research Laboratories. The Netherlands), 1966–

Abstracts for Social Workers (National Association of Social Workers. Albany, New York), 1965–

Abstracts for the Advancement of Industrial Utilization of Wheat (Division of Industrial Research, Washington State University. Pullman, Washington), 1962–

Abstracts from East European Legal Journals, 1964–

Abstracts from Medical Literature Concerning the Use of Music (The Hospitalized Veterans Service of the Musicians Emergency Fund. New York), 1958–

Abstracts in Anthropology (AIA), 1970–

Abstracts in Religious Education: Selected Studies of Weekday Church Schools (International Council of Religious Education, Bureau of Research), 1934–

Abstracts Journal for Metallurgy of USSR, 1958–

Abstracts of Articles Published in Japanese Scientific and Technical Periodicals (Institute of Science and Technology, Academia Sinica. Peking), 1964–

Abstracts of Bacteriology (Society of American Bacteriologists. Baltimore, Md.), 1917–25 (amalgamated with *Botanical Abstracts* to become *Biological Abstracts*)

Abstracts of Bioanalytic Technology (American Association of Bioanalysts. Chicago), 1953–65

Abstracts of Bulgarian Scientific Literature (Centre of Information and Scientific Documentation, Bulgarian Academy of Sciences. Sofia), 1958–

Abstracts of Canning Technology (National Canners Association Research Laboratory. Washington, D.C.), 1923–30

Abstracts of Chemical Papers (Bureau of Chemical Abstracts. London), 1924–25 (continued by *British Abstracts*)

Abstracts of Computer Literature (Burroughs Corporation. Pasadena, Calif.), 1957–

Abstracts of Current Literature on Tuberculosis (Japan Antituberculosis Association. Tokyo), 1950–

Abstracts of Current Literature on Venereal Disease: An Annotated Bibliography (US Communicable Disease Center, Venereal Disease Branch, Atlanta, Ga.), 1952–

Abstracts of Declassified Documents (US Atomic Energy Commission. Oak Ridge, Tenn.), 1947–48 (continued by *Nuclear Science Abstracts*)

Abstracts of Dentistry, 1962–

Abstracts of Efficiency Studies in the Hospital Service, 1961–

Abstracts of English Studies (National Council of Teachers of English. Boulder, Colorado), 1958–

Abstracts of Exploration and Production Literature and Patents (University of Tulsa. Tulsa, Oklahoma), 1969–

Abstracts of Folklore Studies (American Folklore Society. Austin, Texas), 1963–

Abstracts of General Biology, 1964–

Abstracts of Hospital Management Studies (Co-operative Information Center for Hospital Management Studies, University of Michigan. Ann Arbor, Mich.), 1964–

Abstracts of Human Developmental Biology, 1961–62 (continued by *Excerpta Medica*, Section 21: Human Developmental Biology)

Abstracts of Hygiene 1914–

Abstracts of Instructional Developments at CIC Institutions (CIC Committee on Research and Development of Instructional Researches. Ann Arbor, Mich.), 1966–

Abstracts of Instructional Materials in Vocational and Technical Education (ERIC Clearinghouse: The Center for Vocational and Technical Education. Columbus, Ohio), 1967–

Abstracts of Japanese Medicine (Excerpta Medica Foundation. Amsterdam), 1960/61–

Abstracts of Leading Publications in Psychiatric Medicine (Carrier Clinic. Belle Meade, New Jersey), 1958–63

Abstracts of Literature on Milk and Milk Products, 1936–   (included in *Journal of Dairy Science*)

Abstracts of Literature on the Manufacture and Distribution of Ice-Cream (International Association of Ice Cream Manufacturers. Harrisburg, Pa.), 1927–34/35 (continued by *Abstracts of Literature on Milk and Milk Products*)

Abstracts of Music Literature (RILM) (International Repertory of Music Center, Queens College of the City University of New York), 1967–

Abstracts of Mycology, 1967–

Abstracts of New World Archaeology (Society for American Archaeology. Salt Lake City, Utah), 1959–

Abstracts of North American Geology (US Geological Survey, Department of the Interior. Washington, D.C.), 1966–

Abstracts of Original Research (Joint Council on Economic Education. New York), 1960–

Abstracts of Orthopedic Surgery (Office of the US Surgeon General, Department of the Army. Washington, D.C.), 1948–50

Abstracts of Papers of Oral Physiological Studies (Kyoto), 1962–

Abstracts of Papers on Geology of the United Kingdom (Commonwealth Geological Liaison Office. London), 1951–

Abstracts of Photographic Science and Engineering Literature (Department of Graphics, Columbia University, in cooperation with the Society of Photographic Scientists and Engineers), 1962– (continued *Ansco Abstracts* and Eastman Kodak Company's *Monthly Abstract Bulletin*)

Abstracts of Physiological Researches, 1916–

Abstracts of Psychiatry for the General Practitioner (Carrier Clinic. Belle Meade, New Jersey), 1958–63

Abstracts of Recent Published Material on Soil and Water, 1960–

Abstracts of Refining Literature (American Petroleum Institute, New York), 1968–

Abstracts of Refining Patents (American Petroleum Institute. New York), 1961–

Abstracts of Research and Related Materials in Vocational and Technical Education (ERIC Clearinghouse. Center for Vocational and Technical Education. Columbus, Ohio), 1967–

Abstracts of Romanian Technical Literature (Institutul de Documentare Tehnica. Bucarest), 1965–

Abstracts of Scientific and Technical Papers Published in Egypt and Papers Received from Afghanistan, Cyprus, Iran, etc., 1955–

Abstracts of Scientific Literature, 1926–37

Abstracts of "701" Planning Reports (US Department of Housing and Urban Development. Washington, D.C.), 1968–

Abstracts of Soviet Medicine (Excerpta Medica Foundation. Amsterdam and New York), 1957–

Abstracts of Student Theses in City and Regional Planning (American Institute of Planners. Washington, D.C.), 1965–

Abstracts of Swiss Patents (US Business and Defense Services Administration. Washington, D.C.), 1962–

Abstracts of the Electrical Commission Engineers of Japan, 1962–

Abstracts of Tuberculosis (National Tuberculosis Association. Baltimore, Md.), 1917–59

Abstracts of Vitamin Literature (Association of Vitamin Chemists. Chicago), 1947–48 (continued by *Vitamin Abstracts*)

Abstracts of World Medicine (British Medical Association. London), 1947–

Abstracts of World Surgery, Obstetrics, and Gynaecology (British Medical Association. London), 1947–52

Abstracts on Hygiene, 1968–   (continued *Bulletin of Hygiene*)

Abstracts on Military and Aviation Ophthalmology and Visual Sciences, 1900/40–52/54; 1953–

Abstracts on Tuberculosis and Other Respiratory Diseases (National Tuberculosis Association. Brooklyn, New York), 1959– (continued *Tuberculosis Abstracts*)

Acoustics Abstracts, 1967–

Advance Abstracts of Contributions in Fisheries and Aquatic Sciences (Central Marine Fisheries Research Institute. Mandapam), 1967–

African Abstracts/Analyses africanistes (International African Institute, with the assistance of UNESCO), 1950–

Agricultural and Horticultural Engineering Abstracts (National Institute of Agricultural Engineering. Silsoe), 1950–

Agricultural Chemicals/Update, 1969–   (includes abstracts)

Air Pollution Control Association Abstracts/APCA Abstracts, 1955–

Allgemeines Magazin der Natur, Kunst und Wissenschaften, 1753–67

America: History and Life, 1963–

American Association of Variable Star Observers Abstracts/AAVSO Abstracts, 1960–

American Behavioral Scientist, 1957–   (includes abstracts)

American Medical Intelligencer: A Concentrated Record of Medical Science and Literature, 1837–42 (continued by *Medical News*)

American Petroleum Institute Abstracts of Refining Literature/API Abstracts of Refining Literature, 1968–

American Petroleum Institute Abstracts of Transportation and Storage Literature and Patents, 1968–

American Petroleum Institute Abstracts of Petroleum Substitutes Literature and Patents, 1969–

American Society for Metals Review of Metals/ASM Review of Metals, 1944–

American Society of Civil Engineers Publications Abstracts/ASCE Publications Abstracts, 1960–

Analytical Review; or, History of Literature, Domestic and Foreign, 1788–98

Analyses africanistes/African Abstracts (International African Institute, with the assistance of UNESCO), 1950–

Anatomy, Anthropology, Embryology and Histology (*Excerpta Medica,* Section 1), 1947–

Anbar Management Services Abstracts, 1961–

Anesthesiology (*Excerpta Medica,* Section 24), 1966–

Animal Breeding Abstracts (Imperial Bureau of Animal Breeding and Genetics. Edinburgh), 1933–

Animal Husbandry (Helminthological Abstracts, Series A), 1970–

Annales de chimie et de physique, 1789–1815

Annales sociologiques, 1934–42 (continued *L'Année sociologique*)

L'Année philosophique, 1890–1913

L'Année psychologique, 1894–

L'Année sociologique, 1896–1912; 1923–25; 1940/48–   (continued by *Annales sociologiques* during 1934–42)

Annotated Bibliography of Economic Geology, 1929–

Annual Abstract of Statistics (Great Britain), 1840–53–

Ansco Abstracts, 1941–61 (continued by *Abstracts of Photographic Science and Engineering Literature*)

Antarctic Bibliography (Office of Antarctic Programs, National Science Foundation. Washington, D.C.), 1965–

Anthropologischer Anzeiger: Bericht über die biologisch-anthropologische Literatur, 1924–44; 1956–

Apicultural Abstracts (Bee Research Association. London), 1950–

Applied Mechanics Reviews (American Society of Mechanical Engineers), 1962–

Archives de sociologie des religions (Centre national de la recherche scientifique. Paris), 1956– (includes abstracts)

Arctic Bibliography (Arctic Institute of North America. Washington, D.C.), 1953–

Armed Services Technical Information Agency Abstracts/ASTIA Abstracts, 1957–

Arms Control and Disarmament: A Quarterly Bibliography with Abstracts and Annotations (General Reference and Bibliography Divisions, US Library of Congress. Washington, D.C.), 1964–

Arthritis and Rheumatism (*Excerpta Medica,* Section 6B), 1965–

Astronomischer Jahresbericht, 1899– (compiled since 1942 by the Astronomisches Recheninstitut. Heidelberg)

Aufrichtige und unpartheyische Gedancken über die Journale, Extracte und Monaths-Schriften, worinnen dieselben extrahiret, wann es nützlich suppliret oder wo es nothig emediret werden; nebst einer Vorrede von der Annehmlichkeit, Nützen und Fehlern gedachter Schriften, 1714–17

Ausführliche und kritische Nachrichten von den besten und merkwürdigsten Schriften unsrer Zeit, 1763–65 (continued as *Vollständige und kritische Nachrichten . . .*)

Australian Journal of Science, 1922– (includes abstracts)

Australian Social Science Abstracts (Committee on Research in the Social Sciences, Australian National Research Council), 1946–51; (Social Science Council of Australia), 1952–54

Automation Express, 1958–

BBAA: boletín bibliográfico de antropología americana (Instituto Panamericano de geografía e historia. Mexico City), 1937–

BCIRA Abstracts of Foundry Literature (British Cast Iron Research Association. Alvechurch, Birmingham), 1969–

Battelle Technical Review (Battelle Memorial Institute, Columbus, Ohio), 1952–

Beiblätter zu den Annalen der Physik, 1877–

Bibliographia oceanographica (Commissione internazionale per l'esplorazione scientifica del Mare Mediterraneo. Comitato italiano), 1929–56

Bibliographical Bulletin for Welding and Allied Processes (International Institute of Welding), 1949– (continued the *Bulletin de documentation de la soudure*)

Bibliographie agricole et économique, 1950–

Bibliographie de la philosophie (International Institute of Philosophy. Paris), 1937–39; 1946–53

Bibliographie ethnographique de l'Afrique Sud Saharenne (Musée royal de l'Afrique centrale), 1960–

Bibliographie ethnographique de Congo et des régions araisinaltes, 1935–

Bibliographie géologique du Congo et du Ruanda-Urundi, 1918–

Bibliographie géologique du Maroc (Division de la géologie. Rabat), 1960–

Bibliography and Abstracts on Electrical Contacts, 1944–

Bibliography of Scientific and Industrial Reports, 1946–53 (continued as *United States Government Research Reports*)

Biochemistry (*Excerpta Medica*, Section 2B), 1965–

Biological Abstracts, 1926–

Biophysics, Bio-engineering and Medical Instrumentation (*Excerpta Medica*, Section 27), 1969–

BioResearch Index, 1966–

Boletim analitico do Centro de Documentação Científica Ultramarina (Centro de Documentação Científica Ultramarina), 1959–

Boletín bibliográfico de antropología americana (Fondo de cultura economica. Mexico City), 1937–48

Boletín chileno de parasitología (Departamento de Parasitología, Universidad de Chile), 1946–

Bolletino emerográfico di economia internazionale (Istituto di economia internazionale. Genoa), 1948–

Botanischer Jahresbericht (Just's), 1873–

British Abstracts, 1926–53 (continuing the abstracts in the Journals of the Chemical Society, 1871 onwards, and the Society of Chemical Industry, 1882 onwards)

British Archaeological Abstracts (Council for British Archaeology. London), 1968–

British Cast Iron Research Association Abstracts of Foundry Literature / BCIRA Abstracts of Foundry Literature, 1969–

British Ceramic Abstracts, 1950–

Building Science Abstracts (Building Research Station. Garston), 1928–

Bulletin of the International Institute of Refrigeration, 1910–

Bulletin analytique (Centre national de la recherche scientifique. Paris), 1940–55 (continued as the *Bulletin signalétique*)

Bulletin analytique de documentation politique, économique et sociale contemporaine (Fondation nationale des sciences politiques. Paris), 1946–

Bulletin bibliographique de pédologie (Service central documentation, Office de la recherche scientifique et technique d'outre-mer [ORSTOM]. Bondy), 1961–

Bulletin de documentation de la soudure et des techniques connexes, 1948 (continued as the *Bibliographical Bulletin For Welding*)

Bulletin du Bureau minier du Mali, 1962–

Bulletin général et universel des annonces et des nouvelles scientifiques, 1823 (continued by the *Bulletin universel des sciences et de l'industrie*)

Bulletin signalétique (Centre national de la recherche scientifique. Paris), 1956– (continued the *Bulletin analytique*)

Bulletin signalétique d'entomologie médicale et vétérinaire (Service central documentation, Office de la recherche scientifique et technique d'outre-mer [ORSTOM]. Bondy), 1961–

Bulletin universel des sciences et de l'industrie (Société pour la propagation des connaissances scientifiques et industrielles. Paris), 1824–31 (continued the *Bulletin universel des sciences et de l'industrie*)

Business Briefs (Pasadena Public Library), 1970–

CSIRO Abstracts (Commonwealth Scientific and Industrial Research Organization. East Melbourne), 1952–

CSP Abstracts/College Student Personnel Abstracts (College Student Personnel Institute, Claremont, Calif.), 1965–

Cancer (*Excerpta Medica, Section* 16), 1953–

Cancer Abstracts, 1951–

Cancer Chemotherapy Abstracts, 1960–

Cancer Research (American Association for Cancer Research), 1941–

Cardiovascular Diseases (*Excerpta Medica, Section* 18), 1957–

Censure de la censure/Journal du journal, 1670–

Ceramic Abstracts (American Ceramic Society. Columbus, Ohio), 1922–

Ceramic-Metal Systems and Enamel Bibliography, with Abstracts and Indexes (Ceramic-Metal Systems Division, American Ceramic Society), 1960/69–   (continues *Enamel Bibliography and Abstracts*)

Chemical Abstracts (American Chemical Society, Easton, Pa.), 1907–

Chemical Society. Journal, 1871–1925 (included abstracts) (abstracts continued in *British Abstracts*)

Chemisches Zentralblatt (Berlin Academy), 1830–1970 (continued by a *Fortschrittsbericht*)

Chest Disease Index and Abstracts, 1946–65 (continued *Tuberculosis Index*)

Chest Diseases, Thoracic Surgery, and Tuberculosis (*Excerpta Medica, Section* 15), 1969–

Child Development Abstracts and Bibliography (Society for Research in Child Development. Washington, D.C.), 1927–

Chimie analytique (Centre de documentation chimique. Paris), 1896–

Chimie et industrie (Centre de documentation chimique. Paris), 1918–

Chronique de la sécurité industrielle (Industrial Safety Section, International Labour Office. Geneva), 1925–   (includes abstracts)

Ciencias sociales: notas e informaciones (Social Sciences Section, Department of Cultural Affairs, Pan American Union. Washington, D.C.), 1950–

College Student Personnel Abstracts/CSPA Abstracts (College Student Personnel Institute. Claremont, Calif.), 1965–

Commercial Fisheries Abstracts (US Bureau of Commercial Fisheries. Washington, D.C.), 1948–

Commonwealth Scientific and Industrial Research Organization Abstracts/CSIRO Abstracts, 1952–

Communications in Behavioral Biology, Pt. B: Abstracts and Index, 1966–

Communist Chinese Scientific Abstracts, 1965–

Computer Abstracts, 1960–   (continued *Computer Bibliography*)

Computer Bibliography, 1959 (preceded by *Computers;* continued by *Computer Abstracts*)

Computers, 1957–58 (continued as *Computer Bibliography*)

Computing Reviews (Association for Computing Machinery. New York), 1960–

Control Abstracts (Science Abstracts, Section C. Institution of Electrical Engineers, in association with the International Federation of Automatic Control. London), 1966–

Corrosion: Traitements, Protection, Finition, 1967–   (continues *Corrosion et anticorrosion*)

Corrosion Abstracts (Ingeniors Vetenskapsakademien Korrosionsamd. Stockholm), 1966–

Corrosion Abstracts (National Association of Corrosion Engineers. Houston, Texas), 1962–

Corrosion et anticorrosion (Centre de documentation chimique. Paris), 1953–67

Crell's Chemisches Journal, 1778–81 (and similar journals, also issued by Crell, extending to 1791) (continued by the *Neueste Entdeckungen in der Chemie*)

Crerar Metals Abstracts, 1952–

Crime and Delinquency Abstracts (US National Clearinghouse for Mental Health Information.) 1966–   (continued the *International Bibliography on Crime and Delinquency*)

Cybernetics Abstracts, 1964–

DOD Technical Reports (Defense Documentation Center. Alexandria, Va.), 1951–

dsh Abstracts (American Speech and Hearing Association. Washington), 1960–   [*NB:* dsh = deafness, speech, hearing]

Deep-Sea Research and Oceanographic Abstracts, 1953–

Defense Documentation Center Technical Reports/DOD Technical Reports, 1951–

Dental Abstracts (Los Angeles), 1939 (two issues only)

Dental Abstracts (Columbia University), 1941–50

Dental Abstracts (American Dental Association. Chicago), 1956–

Dermatology and Venereology (*Excerpta Medica,* Section 13) 1947–

Deutsche acta eruditorum; oder, Geschichte der Gelehrten, welche den gegenwärtigen Zustand der Literatur in Europa begreiffen, 1712–39 (superseded by the *Zuverlässige Nachrichten . . .*)

Deutscher Zahn-, Mund- und Kieferheilkunde, 1934–43; 1948– (continued the *Zentralblatt für die gesamte Zahn-, Mund- und Kieferheilkunde*)

Developmental Biology and Teratology (Excerpta Medica Foundation. Amsterdam), 1965–   (continued *Human Developmental Biology*)

Dissertation Abstracts, 1938–

Distillers Plastics Abstracts, 1964–

Documentation and Information Science Abstracts (sponsored by the American Documentation Institute, the Division of Chemical Literature of the American Chemical Society, and the Special Libraries Association), 1966–

Documentation économique (Institut national de la statistique et des études économiques. Paris), 1934–38; 1947–

Documentation politique internationale de sciences politique/International Political Science Abstracts (International Political Science Association, and the International Studies Conference), 1951–

Documentieblad (Royal Tropical Institute. Amsterdam), 1946–52 (continued as *Tropical Abstracts*)

ERIC, Research in Education: A Monthly Abstract Journal (Educational Resources Information Center. Washington, D.C.), 1966–

East European Science Abstracts, 1965–

Economic Abstracts (Graduate School of Arts and Science, New York University) 1952–56

Economic Abstracts: Semi-Monthly Review of Abstracts on Economics, Finance, Trade and Industry, Management and Labour (prepared by the Library of the Economic Information Service of the Netherlands Ministry of Economic Affairs, in collaboration with the Library of the Netherlands School of Economics, and the Library of the Ministry of Social Affairs. The Hague), 1953–

Education Abstracts (Albany, New York) 1938–44 (continued *Educational Abstracts*)

Education Abstracts (UNESCO. Paris), 1952–

Educational Abstracts, 1936–37 (continued by *Education Abstracts*)

Educational Administration Abstracts (University Council for Educational Administration. Danville, Ill.), 1966–

Electrical and Electronics Abstracts (Science Abstracts, Section B. Institution of Electrical and Electronics Engineers. London), 1903–

Electroanalytical Abstracts, 1963–   (preceded by a section in the *Journal of Electroanalytical Chemistry*)

Electronics Abstracts Journal, 1966–

Employment Relations Abstracts, 1950–

Enamel Bibliography and Abstracts, 1928–59 (continued by *Ceramic-Metal Systems and Enamel Bibliography . . .*)

Enamelling Abstracts, 1939–43

Endocrinology (*Excerpta Medica,* Section 3), 1947–

Engineering Design Abstracts (Enfield College of Technology), 1966–

Engineering Abstracts, 1910–13 (International Institute of Technical Bibliography. London)

Engineering Abstracts (Institution of Civil Engineers. London), 1919–37

Engineering Index, 1884–

English-Teaching Abstracts (English-Teaching Information Centre, British Council. London), 1961–

Environmental Effects on Materials and Equipment Abstracts, 1962–

Epilepsy Abstracts (National Institute of Neurological Diseases and Blindness), 1967–

Esprit des journaux français et étrangers (Société des gens de lettres de France. Paris), 1772–1815; 1817–18

Eugenics Quarterly (American Eugenics Society. Baltimore, Md.), 1954–
(includes abstracts)

Excerpta Botanica, Sectio A: Taxonomica et chorologica; Sectio B: Sociologica (International Association for Plant Taxonomy. Stuttgart), 1955–

Exerpta Criminologica: An International Abstracting Service Covering the Etiology of Crime and Juvenile Delinquency, the Control and Treatment of Offenders, Criminal Procedure, and the Administration of Justice (Excerpta Criminologica Foundation, in cooperation with the National Council on Crime and Delinquency, the Institute of State and Law of the Academy of Sciences of the USSR, and the National Bureau for Child Protection. The Hague), 1961–

Excerpta Historica Nordica (International Committee of Historical Sciences, Copenhagen), 1955–

Excerpta Medica (Excerpta Medica Foundation. Amsterdam), 1947–

Facts on File, 1940–

Fertilizer Abstracts (Technical Library, National Fertilizer Development Center, TVA), 1968–

Finishing Abstracts, 1964– (included, 1964–68, a "Metal finishing abstracts international trade literature supplement")

Fire Research Abstracts and Reviews, 1958–

Fluidics Feedback: Abstracts from Current Literature (The British Hydromechanics Research Association. Cranfield), 1967–

Food Science and Technology Abstracts (sponsored by the Commonwealth Agricultural Bureaux, the Institut für Dokumentationswesen, and the Institute of Food Technologists), 1969–

Die Fortschritte der Physik, 1845–1918 (continued as the *Physikalische Berichte*)

Fortschritte der Technik, 1909–10 (continued *Repertorium der technischen Journal-Literatur;* continued by *Engineering Abstracts*)

Fortschritte der Zahnheilkunde nebst Literaturarchiv, 1925–33

Fuel Abstracts (Fuel Research Board, DSIR), 1947–

Fuel Abstracts and Current Titles (Institute of Fuel. London), 1945–

Fundamental Education Abstracts (UNESCO Department of Education. Paris), 1949–51 (continued by *Education Abstracts*)

Gaikoku Tokkyo Sokuho [Japanese foreign patent news], 1957–

Gas Abstracts (Institute of Gas Technology. Chicago), 1945–

General Pathology and Pathological Anatomy (*Excerpta Medica,* Section 5), 1948–

Genetics Abstracts, 1968–

Geographical Abstracts (Department of Geography, London School of Economics, University of London), 1966– (in four separate parts: A. Geomorphology; B. Biogeography, climatology, and cartography; C. Economic geography; D. Social geography)

Geographische Büchersall zum Nutzen und Vergnügen eröffnet, 1764–78 (included abstracts)

Geological Abstracts (American Geological Institute. Washington, D.C.), 1953–58 (continued by *GeoScience Abstracts*)

Geomorphological Abstracts, 1960–65 (continued by *Geographical Abstracts,* A. Geomorphology)

Geophysical Abstracts (US Bureau of Mines; subsequently Geological Survey, US Department of the Interior), 1929–

GeoScience Abstracts (American Geological Institute. Washington, D.C.), 1959– (continued *Geological Abstracts*)

Gerontology and Geriatrics (*Excerpta Medica,* Section 20), 1958–

Guide du génie chimique (Centre de documentation chimique. Paris), 1918–

HRIS Abstracts (Highway Research Board. Washington, D.C.), 1968–

Half-Yearly Abstract of the Medical Sciences: Being a Digest of British and Continental Medicine and of the Progress of Medicine and the Collateral Sciences, 1845–73 (continued by *Monthly Abstract Medical Science*)

Health Aspects of Pesticides Abstract Bulletin (US Food and Drug Administration. Washington, D.C.), 1968–

Hematology (*Excerpta Medica,* Section 25), 1967–

Histoire des ouvrages des savans, 1687–1706; 1708–09

Historical Abstracts, 1775–1970 (commencing 1971), 1955–

Human Developmental Biology, 1963–64 (continued *Abstracts of Human Developmental Biology;* continued by *Developmental Biology and Teratology*)

Human Genetics (*Excerpta Medica,* Section 22), 1962–

Hungarian Technical Abstracts (Hungarian Central Technical Library and Documentation Centre. Budapest), 1949–

Immunology, Serology and Transplantation (*Excerpta Medica,* Section 2), 1967–

Index Aeronauticus: Journal of Aeronautical and Astronautical Abstracts (Ministry of Aviation), 1944–

Index and Abstracts of Foreign Physical Education Literature (Phi Epsilon Kappa Fraternity. Indianapolis), 1955–

Indian Education Abstracts (Ministry of Education. New Delhi), 1954–

Indian Science Abstracts (ISA): Annotated Bibliography of Science in India (National Institute of Sciences), 1939–59; (Insdoc. New Delhi), 1965–

Indice histórico español (Universidad de Barcelona, in collaboration with *Historical Abstracts*), 1953–

Indonesian Abstracts (Council for Sciences of Indonesia. Djakarta), 1958–

Industrial Ergonomics Abstracts (British Iron and Steel Research Association. London), 1965–

Industrial Relations Law Digest, 1958–

Industrial Statistics Abstracts/International Journal of Abstracts on Statistical Methods in Industry (International Statistical Institute. The Hague), 1954–

Industrial Training Abstracts (Institute of Personnel Methods, School of Business Administration, Wayne State University. Detroit), 1947–53.

Information Science Abstracts, 1969– (continues *Documentation and Information Science Abstracts*)

Institute of Metals. Journal, 1909–30 (included abstracts—these were continued in *Metallurgical Abstracts*)

Institute of Petroleum Abstracts, 1969–

Institution of Civil Engineers, London. Engineering Abstracts, 1919–37

Instrument Abstracts (British Scientific Instrument Research Association [SIRA]. London), 1946–

Internal Medicine (*Excerpta Medica,* Section 6), 1947–

International Abstracts of Surgery, 1913–   (supplement to *Surgery, Gynecology and Obstetrics*)

International Abstracts in Operations Research (Operations Research Society of America, for the International Federation of Operational Research Societies), 1961–

International Abstracts of Biological Sciences, 1956–   (continued *British Abstracts,* Series A, Section 3)

International Aerospace Abstracts (Technical Information Service, American Institute of Aeronautics and Astronautics.), 1961– (complements *Scientific and Technical Aerospace Reports*)

International Bibliography on Crime and Delinquency (National Clearinghouse for Mental Health Information. Bethesda, Md.), 1964–65 (continued as *Crime and Delinquency Abstracts*)

International Institute of Refrigeration Bulletin, 1910–

International Journal of Abstracts: Statistical Theory and Method (International Statistical Institute. The Hague), 1959–

International Journal of Abstracts on Statistical Methods in Industry/Industrial Statistics Abstracts (International Statistical Institute. The Hague), 1954–

International Pharmaceutical Abstracts (American Society of Hospital Pharmacists), 1964–

International Political Science Abstracts/Documentation politique internationale de sciences politique (International Political Science Association, and the International Studies Conference), 1951–

Inventory of Research in Racial and Cultural Relations (Committee on Education, Training and Research in Race Relations, University of Chicago), 1948–

Iodine Abstracts and Reviews (Chilean Iodine Educational Bureau. New York), 1949–60

Jahrbuch über die Fortschritte der Mathematik, 1868–1944

Japan Science Review: Humanistic Studies (Union of Japanese Societies of Literature, Philosophy and History. Tokyo), 1950–

Japan Science Review: Engineering Sciences (Association for Science Documents Information. Tokyo), 1949–

Journal des journaux, 1760 (Jan.–Apr.)

Journal des sçavans, 1665–1792 (continued by the *Journal des savants*)

Journal des savants (Académie des inscriptions et belles-lettres. Paris), 1797; 1816– (continued the *Journal des sçavans*)

Journal du journal; ou, Censure de la censure, 1670–

Journal encyclopédique ou universel, 1756–93

Journal of Dairy Science (American Dairy Science Association, Lancaster Pa.), 1936–   (includes abstracts section)

Journal of Economic Abstracts (American Economic Association. Cambridge, Mass.), 1963–

Journal of Electroanalytical Chemistry, 1962 (included abstracts. Continued in *Electroanalytical Abstracts*)

Journal of the Chemical Society, 1871–1925 (included abstracts—these were continued in *British Abstracts*)

Journal of the Institute of Metals, 1909–30 (included abstracts—these were continued in *Metallurgical Abstracts*)

Journal of the Society of Chemical Industry, 1882–1925 (included abstracts —these were continued in *British Abstracts*)

Journal of Venereal Disease Information (US Public Health Service. Venereal Diseases Division. Washington, D.C.), 1920–51

Journalism Abstracts (The Association for Education in Journalism. Chapel Hill, N.C.), 1963–

Just's Botanischer Jahresbericht: systematisch geordnetes Repertorium der botanischen Literatur aller Länder, 1873–

Kagaku gijutsu bunken sokuho [Current bibliography of Japanese science and technology], 1959–

Keesing's Contemporary Archives, 1931–   (continued *Synopsis of Important Events*)

LLBA: Language and Language Behavior Abstracts (The University of Michigan Center for Research on Language Behavior [CRLLB], in collaboration with the Bureau pour l'enseignement de la langue et de la civilisation françaises à l'étranger [BELC], Paris), 1967–

Laser Abstracts 1964–

Law Times Reports 1843–1947

Lead Abstracts (Lead Development Association. London), 1958–

Leukemia Abstracts (Research Information Service, the John Crerar Library. Chicago), 1953–

Library Science Abstracts (The Library Association. London), 1950–

Literatur-Verzeichnis der politischen Wissenschaften (Hochschule für politische Wissenschaften. Munich), 1952–

Literature on Automation (IFIP Administrative Data Processing Group, Amsterdam), 1961–

Literature Service: Resins, Rubbers, Plastics, 1946–   (continued *Resins, Rubbers, and Plastics Abstract Service*)

London Shellac Research Bureau. Abstracts Bearing on Shellac Research Literature, 1928/33-44

MIRA Monthly Summary: Abstracts of Automobile Engineering Literature (Motor Industry Research Association, Lindley), 1920–

Machine Science Abstracts, 1965–

Management Abstracts (British Institute of Management, London), 1948–

Massachusetts Institute of Technology. Abstracts of Scientific and Technical Publications, 1928–32.

Masters Abstracts, 1962–

Materials in Design Engineering, 1929–

Mathematical Reviews (American Mathematical Society), 1940–

Medical Instrumentation (*Excerpta Medica*, Section 27), 1967–

Medical Microbiology and Hygiene (*Excerpta Medica*, Section 4), 1948–

Medical News, 1843–1905 (continued *American Medical Intelligencer;* continued by the *New York Medical Journal* and *Medical Record*)

Mental Retardation Abstracts (Division of Mental Rehabilitation, Rehabilitation Services Administration), 1964–

Metal Finishing Abstracts, 1959–64 (continued in *Finishing Abstracts*)

Metal Finishing Plant and Process, 1969– (continues the "Metal finishing abstracts international trade literature supplement" of *Finishing Abstracts*)

Metallurgical Abstracts (Institute of Metals. London), 1931– (continues the abstracts published in the Institute's *Journal*)

Metallurgical Engineering Digest, Ferrous and Non-Ferrous, 1945–

Metals Abstracts, 1968– (continued *Review of Metal Literature*)

Meteorological Abstracts and Bibliography (American Meteorological Society), 1950–59 (continued by *Meteorological and Geoastrophysical Abstracts*)

Meteorological and Geoastrophysical Abstracts (American Meteorological Society), 1960– (continues *Meteorological Abstracts and Bibliography*)

Microbiology: Bacteriology, Virology, Mycology and Parasitology (*Excerpta Medica*, Section 4), 1948–

Mineralogical Abstracts (started by the British Mineralogical Society; published jointly with the American Mineralogical Society since 1961), 1920–

Monatsextracte, 1703–

Monthly Abstract Bulletin (Research Laboratories, Eastman Kodak Company. Rochester, New York), 1915–61 (continued by *Abstracts of Photographic Science and Engineering Literature*)

Monthly Abstract of Medical Science, 1874–79 (continued *Half-Yearly Abstract of the Medical Sciences;* continued by *Medical News and Abstract*)

Monthly Review: A Periodical Work, Giving an Account, with Proper Abstracts of, and Extracts from, the New Books, Pamphlets, & c., As They Come Out, 1749–1844

Monthly Summary of Automobile Engineering Literature (Motor Industry Research Association. Lindley), 1920–

National Council of the Churches of Christ in the USA. Bureau of Research and Survey. Abstracts of Doctoral Dissertations in Religious Education, 1933–

Neue Auszüge aus den besten ausländischen Wochen- und Monatsschriften, 1765–69

Neues Jahrbuch für Mineralogie, Geologie, und Paläontologie, 1807–

Neurology and Neurosurgery (*Excerpta Medica,* Section 8), 1948–

New Testament Abstracts (Weston College School of Theology. Cambridge, Mass.), 1956–

New York Times Index, 1851–

Nihon genshiryoku kenkyujo/Nuclear Science Abstracts of Japan, 1961–

Nippon kagaku soran [Chemical Abstracts of Japan], 1877–

Nouvelles annales de mathématiques: journal des candidats aux écoles polytechnique et normale, 1842–43

Nouvelles de la République des lettres, 1684–1718

Nuclear Medicine (*Excerpta Medica,* Section 23), 1964–

Nuclear Science Abstracts (Division of Technical Information, United States Atomic Energy Commission. Oak Ridge, Tennessee), 1948–

Nuclear Science Abstracts of Japan/Nihon genshiryoku kenkyujo, 1961–

Nuclear Science Abstracts of Poland (Osrodek informacji o energii jadrowej. Warsaw), 1965–

Nutrition Abstracts and Reviews (Commonwealth Bureau of Animal Nutrition. Aberdeen), 1931–

Obstetrics and Gynaecology (*Excerpta Medica,* Section 10), 1947–

Occupational Abstracts, 1965–

Oceanic Index (Oceanic Research Institute. La Jolla, Calif.), 1964–

Official Gazette of the US Patent Office, 1872–

Operations Research/Management Science: An International Literature Digest Service, 1961–

Ophthalmology (*Excerpta Medica,* Section 12), 1947–

Oral Research Abstracts (American Dental Association. Chicago), 1966–

Orthopedic Surgery (*Excerpta Medica,* Section 9), 1956–

Oto-, Rhino-, Larynogology (*Excerpta Medica,* Section 11), 1948–

PHRA: Poverty and Human Resources Abstracts (Institute of Labor and Industrial Relations, University of Michigan—Wayne State University), 1966–

Pakistan Science Abstracts (Pakistan National Scientific and Technical Documentation Centre [PANSDOC]. Karachi), 1961–

Paper and Board Abstracts (PIRA, The Research Association for the Paper and Board, Printing and Packaging Industries. Paper Division. Kenley), 1968–

Parfumerie, cosmétiques, savons (Centre de documentation chimique. Paris), 1918–

Pediatrics (*Excerpta Medica,* Section 7), 1947–

Peintures, pigments, vernis (Centre de documentation chimique. Paris), 1924–

Personnel Management Abstracts (Graduate School of Business Administration, University of Michigan Bureau of Industrial Relations), 1955–

Pesticides Documentation Bulletin (National Agricultural Library), 1965–

Pharmacology and Toxicology (*Excerpta Medica,* Section 18), 1965–

Philippine Abstracts (Division of Documentation, National Institute of Science and Technology. Manila), 1960–

Philippine Series of Specialized Collections of Abstracts (Division of Documentation, National Institute of Science and Technology. Manila), 1960–

The Philosopher's Index, 1969–

Philosophic Abstracts, 1939–54

Photographic Abstracts (Scientific and Technical Group of The Royal Photographic Society of Great Britain), 1920–

Physical Society of London. Abstracts of Physical Papers from Foreign Sources, 1895–97 (continued by *Physics Abstracts*)

Physics Abstracts (Science Abstracts, Section A. Institution of Electrical Engineers. London), 1897–

Physikalische Berichte (Verband Deutscher Physikalischer Gesellschaften), 1920–   (continued *Die Fortschritte der Physik*)

Physiology, Biochemistry, and Pharmacology and Toxicology (*Excerpta Medica*, Section 2), 1948–

Plant Nematology (Helminthological Abstracts, Series B), 1970–

Plastic and Reconstructive Surgery, and the Transplantation Bulletin, 1946–   (includes abstracts)

Plastics Industry Notes (PIN) (Chemical Abstracts Service, Columbus, Ohio), 1970–

Population, II: Notes (Institut national d'études démographiques), 1946–   (includes abstracts)

Poliomyelitis Current Literature (National Foundation for Infantile Paralysis), 1946–

Polymer Science and Technology (POST) (Chemical Abstracts Service, Columbus, Ohio), 1966–

Poverty and Human Resources Abstracts (PHRA) (Institute of Labor and Industrial Relations, University of Michigan—Wayne State University), 1966–

Produits et problèmes pharmaceutiques (Centre de documentation chimique. Paris), 1918–

Psychiatry (*Excerpta Medica,* Section 8), 1948–

Psychological Abstracts (American Psychological Association. Lancaster, Pa.), 1927–   (continued *Psychological Index* from 1937 onwards)

Psychological Index, 1894–1936

Psychopharmacology Abstracts (National Clearinghouse for Mental Health Information. Bethesda, Md.), 1961–

Public Affairs Abstracts (US Library of Congress. Legislative Reference Service. Washington, D.C.), 1945–47; 1950–51

Public Health Bibliographical Series (United States Public Health Service. Washington, D.C.), 1963–   (includes abstracts)

Public Health, Social Medicine, and Hygiene (*Excerpta Medica,* Section 17), 1955–

RILM Abstracts of Music Literature (International Repertory of Music Center, Queen's College of the City University of New York), 1967–

Radiology (*Excerpta Medica,* Section 14), 1947–

Railway Engineering Abstracts (Institution of Civil Engineers. London), 1946–

Ranking's Half-Yearly Abstract of the Medical Sciences, 1845–73 (continued by *Monthly Abstract of Medical Science*)

Reader's Digest, 1922–

Referativnyi zhurnal (Institut Nauchnoi Informatsii, Akademiia Nauk SSSR. Moscow), 1953–

Refrigeration Abstracts (American Society of Refrigeration Engineers, in collaboration with the Refrigeration Research Foundation), 1946–57

Rehabilitation and Physical Medicine (*Excerpta Medica*, Section 19), 1958–

Religious and Theological Abstracts, 1958–

Repertorium der technischen Journal-Literatur, 1856–1908 (retrospective to 1823) (continued by *Fortschritte der Technik*)

Research in Education (ERIC) (Educational Research Information Center. Washington, D.C.), 1966–

Research into Higher Education Abstracts (Society for Research into Higher Education. London), 1967–

Resins, Rubbers, and Plastics Abstract Service, 1942–45 (continued by *Literature Service: Resins, Rubbers, Plastics*)

Resúmenes analíticos de bibliografía militar / Abstracts of Military Bibliography (Instituto de publicaciones navales, Centro Naval. Buenos Aires), 1967–

Review of Metal Literature, 1944–67 (continued by *Metals Abstracts*)

Revue bibliographique de Sinologie (Ecole pratique des hautes études, VIe section. Paris), 1955–

Revue des études islamiques, 1927–   (includes abstracts)

Revue internationale des sciences administratives / International Review of Administrative Sciences (International Institute of Administrative Sciences. Brussels), 1928–   (includes abstracts)

Rheology Abstracts (British Society of Rheology. London), 1958–

Road Abstracts (Road Research Laboratory. Crowthorne), 1934–

Royal Aeronautical Society. Abstracts from the Scientific and Technical Press, 1927–

SIAM Review (Society for Industrial and Applied Mathematics. Philadelphia), 1959–

Sankhyā: The Indian Journal of Statistics (Indian Statistical Institute. Calcutta), 1933–   (includes abstracts in Series A)

Sciences Abstract: Section A. Physics Abstracts, 1897–   ; Section B. Electrical Engineering Abstracts, 1903–   ; Section C. Control Abstracts, 1966–   (Institution of Electrical Engineers. London)

Science Abstracts of China: Mathematics and Physical Science (Institute of Sciences and Technical Information of China. Peking), 1963–

Science Abstracts of China: Technical Sciences (Institute of Sciences and Technical Information of China. Peking), 1963–

Scientia (Universidad Técnica Federico Santa Maria. Valparaiso), 1934–

Scientific and Technical Aerospace Reports (United States National Aeronautics and Space Administration (NASA). Washington, D.C.), 1963–   (continued *Technical Publications Announcements*)

Selected RAND Abstracts (Rand Corporation. Santa Monica, Calif.), 1963–

Selective Soviet Annotated Bibliographies: Asia, Africa, and Latin America, 1961 (continued as *Soviet Periodical Abstracts: Asia, Africa, and Latin America*)

Selective Soviet Annotated Bibliographies: Soviet Society, 1961 (continued as *Soviet Periodical Abstracts: Soviet Society*)

Semiconductor Electronics, 1957–60 (continued by *Solid State Abstracts*)

Social Science Abstracts (Social Science Research Council. Menasha, Wis.), 1928–32

Society for Industrial and Applied Mathematics (SIAM) Review, 1959–

Society of Chemical Industry Journal, 1882–1925 (included abstracts—continued by *British Abstracts*)

Sociologica (*Excerpta Botanica*, Sectio B), 1959–

Sociological Abstracts, 1952–

Sociology of Education Abstracts (School of Education, University of Liverpool), 1965–

Solid State Abstracts, 1960–67 (continued *Semiconductor Electronics*)

South Asia Social Science Abstracts (UNESCO Research Centre on the Social Implications of Industrialisation in Southern Asia. Calcutta), 1952–59 (merged with *South Asia Social Science Bibliography* in 1959 to become *Southern Asia Social Science Bibliography*)

Southern Asia Social Science Bibliography, 1959–65 (continued *South Asia Social Science Abstracts* and *South Asia Social Science Bibliography*)

Soviet Periodical Abstracts: Asia, Africa and Latin America (Slavic Languages Research Institute. New York), 1962– (continued *Selective Soviet Annotated Bibliographies: Asia, Africa, and Latin America*)

Soviet Periodical Abstracts: Soviet Society (Slavic Languages Research Institute. New York), 1961– (continued *Selective Soviet Annotated Bibliographies: Soviet Society*)

Sport Fishery Abstracts: An Abstracting Service for Fishery Research and Management (United States Bureau of Sport Fisheries and Wildlife. Washington, D.C.), 1955–

Standardization Abstracts, 1957–

State and Metropolitan Planning Abstracts (The American Institute of Planners. Washington, D.C.), 1967–

Statistica (published under the auspices of the Universities of Bologna, Padua, and Palermo), 1941– (includes abstracts)

Statistical Abstract of the United States (United States Bureau of the Census. Washington, D.C.), 1878–

Statistical Theory and Method Abstracts (International Statistical Institute, The Hague), 1959–

Surgery (*Excerpta Medica*, Section 9), 1947–

Synopsis of Important Events, 1918–31 (continued by *Keesing's Contemporary Archives*)

Synthetic Liquid Fuels Abstracts (US Office of Synthetic Liquid Fuels. Washington, D.C.), 1944–51

Taxonomica et chorologica (*Excerpta Botanica,* Sectio A) (International Association for Plant Taxonomy. Stuttgart), 1955–
Technical Abstract Bulletin (United States Armed Services Technical Information Agency [ASTIA]. Arlington, Va.), 1957–
Technical Abstract Bulletin (High Duty Alloys, Ltd. Slough), 1933–
Technical Abstracts (Washington, D.C.), 1942–
Technical Education Abstracts (National Foundation for Educational Research. London), 1961–
Technical Information Pilot (United States Library of Congress, Science and Technology Project, for the US Office of Naval Information), 1948–
Technical Publications Announcements (United States National Aeronautics and Space Administration [NASA]. Washington, D.C.), 1962 (continued by *Scientific and Technical Aerospace Reports*)
Theoretical Chemical Engineering Abstracts, 1964–
Thermal Abstracts (Heating and Ventilation Research Association. Bracknell), 1966–
The Times Official Index, 1908–
The Times Law Reports, 1884–1952
Tissue Culture Abstracts, 1964–
Titanium Abstract Bulletin (Imperial Chemical Industries. London), 1955–62
Tobacco Abstracts (North Carolina Agricultural Experiment Station. Tobacco Literature Service. Raleigh, N.C.), 1957–
Tropical Abstracts (Royal Tropical Institute. Amsterdam), 1953– (continued *Documentieblad*)
Tuberculosis and Pulmonary Diseases (*Excerpta Medica,* Section 15), 1948–
Tuberculosis Abstracts (National Tuberculosis Association. Brooklyn, N.Y.), 1928–58 (continued by *Abstracts on Tuberculosis and other Respiratory Diseases*)
L'URSS et les pays de l'Est (Centre de recherches sur l'URSS et les pays de l'Est. Strasbourg University), 1960–
USSR Abstracts of Metallurgy, 1957–
United States Government Research and Development Reports, 1965– (continued *United States Government Research Reports*)
United States Government Research Reports, 1954–64 (continued *Bibliography of Scientific and Industrial Reports*)
United States Statistical Abstract (US Bureau of the Census), 1878–
Universal Magazine of Knowledge and Pleasure, 1747–1815
Update/Agricultural Chemicals, 1969–   (includes abstracts)
Urology and Nephrology (*Excerpta Medica,* Section 28), 1967–
La vie scientifique de l'Université (in *Annales de l'Université de Paris*), 1930–
Virology Abstracts, 1967–
Vitamin Abstracts (Association of Vitamin Chemists. Chicago), 1949– (continued *Abstracts of Vitamin Literature*)
Vollständige Einleitung in die Monaths-Schriften der Deutschen, 1747–

Vollständige und kritische Nachrichten von dem besten und merkwürdigsten Schriften unsrer Zeit, nebst andern zur Gelehrsamkeit gehörigen
Sachen, 1765–69 (continued *Ausführliche und kritische Nachrichten . . .*)

Water Pollution Abstracts (Water Pollution Research Laboratory. London), 1928–

Wheat Abstracts 1962–65

Wildlife Disease (Wildlife Disease Association), 1959–   (includes supplement of abstracts of its contents)

Wildlife Review: An Abstracting Service for Wildlife Management (United
States Fish and Wildlife Service. Laurel, Md.), 1935–

World Agricultural Economics and Rural Sociology Abstracts (The International Association of Agricultural Librarians and Documentalists, in
collaboration with the International Conference of Agricultural Econo-
mists), 1959–

World in Focus (Library of International Relations. Chicago), 1945–

ZDA Abstracts (Zinc Development Association. Oxford), 1943–

Zentralblatt für die gesamte Zahn-, Mund- und Kieferheilkunde, 1936–47
(continued as the *Deutsche Zahn-, Mund- und Kieferheilkunde*)

Zentralblatt für Geologie und Paläontologie, 1950–

Zentralblatt für Mathematik und ihre Grenzgebiete, 1931–44; 1948–

Zentralblatt für Mineralogie, 1950–

Zinc Abstracts/ZDA Abstracts (Zinc Development Association. Oxford),
1943–

Zuverlässige Nachrichten von dem gegenwärtigen Zustande, Veränderung und dem Wachsthum der Wissenschaften, 1740–57

SELECTED READINGS ON ABSTRACTS AND ABSTRACTING SERVICES

Abstracting Scientific and Technical Reports of Defense-Sponsored RDT and E. Washington, D.C., Defense Documentation Center, March 1968 (AD 667 000)

Abstracting Services in Science, Technology, Medicine, Agriculture, Social Sciences, Humanities. The Hague, International Federation for Documentation, 1965 (FID 372) [revised edition published in 1970 in two volumes]

"Abstracts: A Policy Statement." (in *Studies in Philology,* vol. LXIV, no. 5, October 1967, pp. 735-43)

Adams, Scott *and* Baker, Dale B. "Mission and Discipline Orientation in Scientific Abstracting and Indexing Services." (in *Library Trends,* vol. 16, no. 3, January 1968, pp. 307-22)

Anderson, Marian P. *Bibliographic, Indexing, Abstracting and Current Activity Sources: A Guide for Their Use in Mental Health Program Planning.* Sacramento, State of California Department of Mental Hygiene, November 1964.

Bernier, Charles L. "Abstracts and Abstracting." (in *Encyclopedia of Library and Information Science,* vol. 1, 1968, pp. 16-38)

Biosis: Yesterday-Today-Tomorrow. Philadelphia, Biosciences Information Service of Biological Abstracts, 1968.

Boehm, Eric H. *Blueprint for Bibliography: A System for the Social Sciences and Humanities.* Santa Barbara, Calif., Clio Press, 1965.

Boehm, Eric H. "Dissemination of Knowledge in the Humanities and Social Sciences." (in *ACLS Newsletter,* vol. XIV, May 1963, pp. 3-12)

Bohm, E. *Investigation on Nuclear 'Core Journals.'* Brussels, Euratom, 1968 (EUR 3887e)

Borko, Harold *and* Chatman, Seymour. "Criteria for Acceptable Abstracts: A Survey of Abstractors' Instructions." (in *American Documentation,* 14, April, 1963, pp. 149-60)

Brandhorst, W. T. *and* Eckert, P. F. *Guide to the Processing, Storage, and Retrieval of Bibliographic Information at the NASA Scientific and Technical Information Facility.* Springfield, Va., Clearinghouse for Federal Scientific and Technical Information, 1966 (CR-62033)

Bristow, J. S. "Metallurgical Abstracts." (in *Special Libraries,* 52 (10), December 1961, pp. 566-569)

Brodman, Estelle. *Development of Medical Bibliography.* Baltimore, Medical Library Association, 1954 (Medical Library Association, Publication no. 1) (pp. 127-131)

Brodsky, G. L. "Abstracting Control." (in *Technical Information Center Administration,* edited by Arthur W. Elias, 1964, I: pp. 57-71)

Budington, William S. "Crerar Metals Abstracts." (in *Special Libraries,* 52 (10), December 1961, pp. 574-575)

Burchinal, L. G. *and* Haswell, H. A. "How to Put Two and a Half Tons of Research into One Handy Little Box." (in *American Education,* vol. II, February 1966, pp. 23-25)

Burkett, Jack. "Published Indexing and Abstracting Services." (in Burkett, Jack, ed. *Trends in Special Librarianship,* 1968. pp. 35-72)

Chemical Abstracts. *Directions for Abstractors and Section Editors of Chemical Abstracts.* Columbus, Ohio, American Chemical Society, 1960.

Crane, E. J. *A Guide to the Literature of Chemistry.* 2nd edition. 1957 (pp. 123-150, *Abstract Journals*)

Climenson, W. D. *and others.* "Automatic Syntax Analysis in Machine Indexing and Abstracting." (in *American Documentation,* 12 (3) 1961, pp. 178-83.)

Compared Activities of the Main Abstracting and Indexing Services Covering Physics, Chemistry and Biology During the Year 1965. Paris, International Council of Scientific Unions, July 1967.

Cortelyou, Ethaline. "The Abstract of the Technical Report." (in *Journal of Chemical Education,* vol. 8 (4) 1955, pp. 532-33).

"ERIC Guidelines for Abstracting." (in *ERIC Operating Manual.* Washington, D.C., Educational Resources Information Center, 1967. Section 3.4.2.)

Edmundson, H. P. *and* Wyllys, R. E. "Automatic Abstracting and Indexing— Survey and Recommendations." (in *Communications of the ACM,* 4 (5), 1961, pp. 226-234).

Edmundson, H. P. *and others. Automatic Indexing and Abstracting of the Contents of Documents.* Los Angeles, Planning Research Corp., 31 Oct. 1959.

Edmundson, H. P. "Problems in Automatic Abstracting." (in *Communications of the ACM,* 7 (4), 1964, pp. 259-263).

Elliott, C. K. "Abstracting Services in Psychology: A Comparison of 'Psychological Abstracts' and 'Bulletin signalétique.' " (in *Library Association Record,* 71 (9), September 1969, pp. 279-280).

Excerpta Medica: The World-Wide Medical Automated Information Network. Excerpta Mark I System. Amsterdam & New York, Excerpta Medica Foundation, 1969.

"The Formation of Abstracts by the Section of Sentences." (in *American Documentation,* 12 (2), 1961, pp. 139-43).

Forum on the Abstracting and Indexing of Petroleum Exploration and Production Literature, Dallas, 19 February 1960. Special Libraries Association, Petroleum Section, 1961.

Frauendorfer, Sigmund von. *Survey of Abstracting Services and Current Bibliographical Tools in Agriculture, Forestry, Fisheries, Nutrition,*

Veterinary Medicine, and Related Subjects. Munich, Basle, and Vienna, BLV Verlags gesellschaft, 1968.

Garfield, Eugene *and* Sher, I. H. *Article-by-Article Coverage of Selected Abstracting Services.* Philadelphia, Institute for Scientific Information, 1964.

Gibson, Robert W. "The Battelle Technical Review." (in *Special Libraries,* 52 (10), December, 1961, pp. 576-577).

Gray, D. E. *and* Bray, R. S. "Abstracting and Indexing Services of Physics Interest." (in *American Journal of Physics,* May & Dec. 1950, pp. 274-299, 578-579).

Greer, R. C. *and* Atherton, Pauline. *Study of Nuclear Science Abstracts and Physics Abstracts Coverage of Physics Journals,* 1964–1965. New York, American Institute of Physics, 1966.

Guide for the Preparation and Publication of Synopses. Paris, UNESCO, 1962.

Guide for the Preparation of Scientific Papers for Publication. Paris, UNESCO, 1968 (pp. 5-6: "Guide for the Preparation of Authors' Abstracts for Publication")

Guide to Medlars Service. Bethesda, Md., National Library of Medicine, November 1966.

Gulick, Melba C. "Nonconventional Data Sources and Reference Tools for Social Sciences and Humanities." (in *College and Research Libraries,* May, 1968, pp. 224-34).

Herling, John P. "Engineering Abstracting Services." (in *Special Libraries,* 52 (10) December 1961, pp. 560-565).

Herner, S. "Subject Slanting in Scientific Abstracting Publications." (in *International Conference on Scientific Information,* 1960, Area II, pp. 407-427).

Hoshovsky, A. G. "Suggested Criteria for Titles, Abstracts and Index Terms." (in DOD *Technical Reports,* Alexandria, Va., Defense Documentation Center (AD 622 944)

Hyslop, Marjorie R. "ASM Review of Metal Literature." (in *Special Libraries,* 52 (10) December, 1961, pp. 569-571).

Index Bibliographicus: Directory of Current Periodical Abstracts and Bibliographies. Paris, UNESCO, 1968.

Information Retrieval in Action. Cleveland, Ohio, Western Reserve University Press. 1963.

International Federation for Documentation (FID), *1965 Congress, 10-15 October 1965, Washington, D.C. Abstracts.* Washington, D.C., 1965.

International Organization for Standardization. "Abstracts and Synopses." November, 1961 (ISO recommendation R214).

Jacobus, David, *and others.* "Direct User Access to the Biological Literature Through Abstracts." (in *BioScience,* vol. 16, September 1966, pp. 599-603).

Jensen, Raymond A. "The Function of the National Federation of Science Abstracting and Indexing Services." (in *Special Libraries,* 52 (10), December 1961, pp. 555-557).

Juhasz, Stephen, ed. *MAMMAX: Machine-Made and Machine Aided Index.* The National Federation of Science Abstracting and Indexing Services Annual Meeting, Philadelphia, March 1967. San Antonio, Texas, Applied Mechanics Reviews, Southwest Research Institute, 1967 (AMR Report, no. 47).

Karel, L., *and others.* "Computerized Bibliographic Services for Biomedicine." (in *Science,* 184 (3671), May 1965, pp. 766-772).

Keenan, Stella. "Abstracting and Indexing Services in the Physical Sciences." (in *Library Trends,* vol. 16, 1968, pp. 329-336).

Keenan, Stella, *and* Atherton, Pauline. *The Journal Literature of Physics: A Comprehensive Study based on Physics Abstracts 1961 Issues.* New York, American Institute of Physics, 1964.

Keller, Mark. "Documentation of the Alcohol Literature: A Scheme for an Interdisciplinary Field of Study." (in *Quarterly Journal of Studies in Alcohol,* vol. XXV, December 1964, pp. 725-741).

Klempner, Irving M. *Diffusion of Abstracting and Indexing Services for Government-Sponsored Research.* Metuchen, N.J., Scarecrow Press, 1968.

Lewenz, G. F. *and others.* "Style and Speed in Publishing Abstracts." (in *Chemical Documentation,* 1 (2), July 1961, pp. 48-51).

Luhn, H. P. "The Automatic Creation of Literature Abstracts." (in *IBM Journal of Research and Development,* vol. 2 (2), 1958, pp. 159-165)

The Mark II Information Retrieval System; American Society of Metals Documentation System. Metals Park, Ohio, ASM, November 1966.

Maron, M. E. "Automatic Indexing: An Experimental Inquiry." (in *Journal of the ACM,* 8 (3), July 1961, pp. 404-417).

Martyn, John. "Tests on Abstracts Journals: Coverage, Overlap and Indexing." (in *Journal of Documentation,* vol. 23 (1), March 1967, pp. 45-70).

Mayer, Claudius F. "Abstracting and Review Journals" (in Sarton, George, *A Guide to the History of Science.* Waltham, Mass., Chronica Botanica, 1952, pp. 105-110).

Michaelson, Herbert. "Achieving More Disciplined R & D Literature" (in *Journal of Chemical Documentation,* vol. 8 (4), 1968, pp. 198-201).

Mohlman, J. W. "Costs of an Abstracting Program." (in *Journal of Chemical Documentation,* vol. 1, 1961, pp. 64-67).

Mohrhardt, Foster E., ed. "Science Abstracting Services—Commercial, Institutional and Personal." (in *Library Trends,* vol. 16 (3), January 1968, pp. 303-418).

Murphy, Robert L., ed. *ASTIA Guidelines for Cataloging and Abstracting.* Arlington, Va., Armed Services Technical Information Agency, June 1962.

National Federation of Science Abstracting and Indexing Services. *A Guide to the World's Abstracting and Indexing Services in Science and Technology.* Washington, D.C., 1963 (Report no. 102).

Oldsen, Carl F. *Abstractors Manual* (revised edition). East Lansing, Michigan, USOE/MSU Regional Instructional Materials Center for Handicapped Children and Youth, 1969 (includes abstracts for audio-visual materials).

Parkins, Phyllis V. "BioSciences Information Service." (in *Science,* 152 (3724), 1966, pp. 889-894)—includes a history of *Biological Abstracts.*

Postell, Paul E. "Nuclear Science Abstracts." (in *Special Libraries,* 52 (10), December 1961, pp. 572-574).

Reuck, Anthony de *and* Knight, Julie, eds. *Communication in Science: Documentation and Automation.* A Ciba Foundation volume. London, Churchill, 1967.

Ricks, Christopher. "Learned Journals." (in *The Times Literary Supplement,* 4 July 1968, p. 709).

Ripperger, E. A., *and others.* "WADEX (Word Author inDEX): A New Tool in Literature Retrieving." (in *Mechanical Engineering,* March 1964, pp. 45-50).

Ruggles, Melville J. "Bibliography, Indexing, and Abstracting." (in Ruggles, Melville J. *Soviet Libraries and Librarianship.* Chicago, ALA, 1962, pp. 19-36).

Sastri, Madugula I. "Prepositions in *Chemical Abstracts*: A Sememic Study." (in *Linguistics,* vol. 38, 1968, pp. 42-51).

Schultz, Louise. "New Developments in Biological Abstracting and Indexing." (in *Library Trends,* vol. 16, 1968, pp. 337-352).

Scientific and Technical Communication: A Pressing National Problem and Recommendations for its Solution. A report by the Committee on Scientific and Technical Communication of the National Academy of Sciences—National Academy of Engineering. Washington, D.C., National Academy of Sciences, 1969 (pp. 53-57, 130-175).

Shera, Jesse H. *Documentation and the Organization of Knowledge.* London, Crosby Lockwood; Hamden, Conn., Archon Books, 1966.

Siegmann, Philip J. *and* Griffith, Belver C. "The Changing Role of *Psychological Abstracts* in Scientific Communication." (in *American Psychologist,* vol. 21, November 1966, pp. 1037-1043).

Simmons, G. W. "Centralized Abstracting of Petroleum Literature and Patents." (in *Journal of Chemical Documentation,* vol. 5, no. 3, August 1965, pp. 166-69).

Smyth, Virginia M. *and* Brenner, E. H. "The Evolution of Petroleum Abstracts." (in *Special Libraries,* vol. 52 (10), December 1961, pp. 558-560).

Speight, F. Y., ed. *Guide for Source Indexing and Abstracting of the Engineering Literature.* New York Engineers' Joint Council, 1967.

The Study for Automatic Abstracting, C107–IU12. Final report, Canoga Park, Ca., Thomson Ramo Woolridge Inc., 1961. 2 vols.

System Development Corporation. *A System Study of Abstracting and Indexing in the United States.* Falls Church, Va., December 1966. (Technical Memorandum, TM-WD-394-PB 174 249.)

Tate, Fred A. *and* Wood, James L. "Libraries and Abstracting and Indexing Services: A Study in Interdependency." (in *Library Trends,* vol. 16, no. 3, January 1968, pp. 353-374).

Wahl, Richard A. "Patent Abstracts." (in *Official Gazette of the United States Patent Office,* 862 (3), 1969, pp. 653-654).

Weil, B. H., *and others. Technical-Abstracting Fundamentals* (in *Journal of Chemical Documentation,* vol. 3, 1963, pp. 86-89, 125-136).

Welt, Isaac D. "Abstracting and Indexing: An Experimental Course." (Presented before the Documentation Section, Special Libraries Association, New York Meeting, May 31, 1967).

Whaley, F. R. "What the Indexer-Abstractor Does." (in *IEEE Student Journal,* vol. 2 (6), November 1964, pp. 22-24).

Whittingham, D. J. *and others.* "Computerized-Based Subject Index Support Systems Chemical Abstracts Service." (in *Journal of Chemical Documentation,* vol. 6, 1966, pp. 230-234).

World Literature in Physics as Seen through Bulletin Signalétique, 1964 issues. Paris, Conseil international des unions scientifiques, Bureau des résumés analytiques, 1967. 2 volumes.

World Scientific and Technical Literature. Moscow, VINITI, 1969–   (to be completed in 7 volumes).

Wyllys, Ronald E. "Extracting and Abstracting by Computer." (in Borko, Harold. *Automated Language Processing,* New York, Wiley, 1967, pp. 127-179).

INDEX

Articles in professional review journals, or notes in journals of abstracts designed to keep specialists in touch with the literature of their particular fields of interest, can become mere catalogues, sometimes prepared by secretaries who are not research scientists, in which no attempt is made to differentiate good papers from bad, or in which the emphasis is often laid on papers which—regardless of their own scientific or technical merit—support the particular views of the reviewer.

SIR SOLLY ZUCKERMAN

INDEX